THE LIBERTY OF SERVANTS

THE LIBERTY OF SERVANTS

BERLUSCONI'S ITALY

MAURIZIO VIROLI

Translated by
ANTONY SHUGAAR
with a new preface by the author

PRINCETON UNIVERSITY PRESS

PRINCETON AND OXFORD

Original edition published under the title *La libertà dei servi* by Maurizio Viroli
Copyright 2010 by Guis. Laterza & Figli. All rights reserved.
Published by arrangement with Marco Vigevani Agenzia Letteraria
English translation copyright © 2012 by Princeton University Press

Requests for permission to reproduce material from this work should be sent to
Permissions, Princeton University Press

Published by Princeton University Press, 41 William Street, Princeton,
New Jersey 08540
In the United Kingdom: Princeton University Press, 6 Oxford Street,
Woodstock, Oxfordshire OX20 1TW
press.princeton.edu

Jacket Art: Detail of *The Janssen portrait of Shakespeare*, c. early 1610's. Oil
on panel; 55.9 x 43.4 cm. Courtesy of the Folger Shakespeare Library.
Jacket Photograph: Detail of *Italy's Prime Minister Silvio Berlusconi*.
September 19, 2008. Alberto Pizzoli/AFP/Getty images.

Library of Congress Cataloging-in-Publication Data

Viroli, Maurizio.
[Libertà dei servi. English]
The liberty of servants : Berlusconi's Italy / Maurizio Viroli ; translated by Antony
Shugaar with a new preface by the author.
   p. cm.
Originally published in Italian under the title: La liberta dei servi.
Includes bibliographical references and index.
ISBN 978-0-691-15182-3 (hardcover : alk. paper) 1. Italy—Politics and
government—21st century. 2. Political corruption—Italy. 3. Social ethics—
Italy. 4. Political ethics—Italy. 5. Liberty—Italy. 6. Berlusconi, Silvio, 1936–
I. Shugaar, Antony. II. Title.
JN5641.V5713 2011
320.945—dc23   2011026012

British Library Cataloging-in-Publication Data is available

This book has been composed in Minion Pro

Printed on acid-free paper. ∞

Printed in the United States of America

1 3 5 7 9 10 8 6 4 2

To
GIUSEPPE LATERZA,
friend and publisher

The incompetence and the tendency to ignore the letter of the law are intertwined: in order to remain in power, Berlusconi needs menservants, who may possess the quality of obedience, but who are rarely well educated. Their skill is to serve. Anyone who possesses any worth and skill cannot fully be a servant, and will therefore not last long in Berlusconi's employment. I told a friend of mine who went with Berlusconi: Look, it won't be enough for you to bow to him. Now he understands that I was right, but I no longer speak to him. My friendship with my fellow man comes to an end when I see him enter into servitude. At that point, disdain comes into play.

—Paolo Sylos Labini, *Ahi serva Italia*

Contents

❧

Foreword

I wrote this book at the suggestion and with the encouragement of Ian Malcolm, an editor at Princeton University Press, who asked me to explain to an English-speaking audience what is happening in Italian politics. The publisher Giuseppe Laterza bears responsibility for the book coming out first in Italian. He persuaded me by suggesting a title, *La libertà dei servi*—The Liberty of Servants—that synthesizes in a way that cannot be improved upon the ideas that I am setting forth here.

I do believe that Italy is a free country, in the sense that there is liberty, but it is the liberty of servants, not the liberty of citizens. The liberty of servants or of subjects consists in not being hindered in the pursuit of our own ends. The liberty of a citizen, instead, consists in not being subjected to the arbitrary or enormous power of one or several men. Given that an enormous power has established itself in Italy, we are therefore—by the sheer fact that such a power exists—in the condition of servants. The power in question is that of Silvio Berlusconi, possessor of immense wealth; proprietor of television networks, newspapers and magazines, and publishing houses; the founder and the master of a political party that is his to control as he pleases. Such vast power, which has never existed within the liberal and democratic institutions of any other country, engenders what I have described as a court system, that is to say, a form of power characterized by the fact that one man is placed above and at the center of a relatively large number of individuals—his courtiers—who depend on him to gain and preserve wealth, status, and reputation.

I hope to explore, with what will ideally be profitable results, a brilliant insight first set forth by Giovanni Sartori: "There are any number of things by now that frighten me; but the level of submissiveness and intellectual blight manifested on this occasion [the approval of the Alfano Law that ensured the prime minister could count on a suspension of all criminal proceedings against the highest officers of the state] by a majority of our 'honorable' members of parliament frightens me more than anything else. It's as if they were housekeepers. This is not bipartisan cooperation! This is a sultanate, the worst of all courts."[1] The principal characteristic of a court system is its ability to spread or reinforce servile attitudes and habits: adulation, simulation, cynicism, disdain for free spirits, venality, and corruption. If we add to these unhappy results the fact that a man with enormous power can easily make himself master of the laws, we can understand that where a court has formed, the liberty of the citizen cannot exist.

I have wondered—especially in view of the English-language edition of this book—why it was in Italy of all places that we have witnessed the successful political experiment of transforming—without violence—a democratic republic into a court at the center of which sits a *signore*[2] surrounded by a plethora of courtiers, who are in turn admired and envied by a multitude of individuals with servile souls. The answer that strikes me as most plausible is that all this is the product of Italy's longtime moral weakness (in spite of the examples of greatness that have honored our past and our present). By moral weakness I mean the quality that so many political writers have explicated, that is to say, a lack of self-esteem that in some cases masks itself with arrogance, and which makes men willing to become dependent on other men. If I believe that I am not worth much, why should I not serve the powerful, if I profit considerably thereby?

Alongside this cause of a general nature, or context, we should also keep in mind, if we wish to understand what has happened in Italy, what I call "the betrayal of the elite," that is to say, the inability of the political, intellectual, and entrepreneurial elite of Italy to prevent the formation of the enormous power of one man that has destroyed the liberty of the citizens. It is open to discussion whether it might have been possible to prevent things from winding up the way they did, just as it is possible to argue about the most serious mistakes made by this or that political leader. We should and we must discuss whether the lack of wisdom was greater than the lack of will. But what counts in the end are the facts and the facts are undeniable: those whose duty it was to defend the integrity of the Italian Republic failed to do so. I have resisted the temptation to end the essay with predictions on the future of Italian politics. Instead, I have preferred to venture a few considerations, which I hope may prove to be useful, for those who might be interested in working to defeat the court system and help to restore in its place the liberty of citizens. Because, in my opinion, the root cause of the Italian problem can be found in the mores and not in the institutions, much less in the Italian Constitution. I have therefore proposed remedies that are above all ethical in nature. Foremost among them is an attempt to teach a disdain for the court and love of true free living, as well as providing examples of intransigence. There is an abundance of elements in my prescription that make this book very distant from the sensibilities and the way of thinking that prevail in Italy these days.

As out of step with the times as my recommendations may be, my analysis is even more so. The argument that I set forth entails on the part of my readers an acceptance of the republican conception of political liberty, an ideal that enjoyed a long and noble history in Italy but which has since been entirely forgotten or overlooked. Aware of this state of affairs, I originally planned only to publish this book in English. As I mentioned, however, Giuseppe Laterza persuaded me to write it in Italian as well. Whatever becomes of it, I thank him, now that I have finished writing, for having read the first draft and offering a number of excellent suggestions. Likewise I thank all those who have come to my assistance with advice and criticism, foremost among them Fernanda Gallo, Marcello Gisondi, Giorgio Volpe, and my wife Gabriella.

Preface

English speaking readers already have a precise picture of Berlusconi's Italy. Scholars and journalists have accurately documented and explained that Berlusconi's system of power has no precedent and no equal in the history of liberal and democratic countries. Never has a man with so much power—based on wealth, ownership of a media empire, and control of party of people faithful to him personally—been able to become head of government for three times and to assume a central and dominating position for fifteen years.[1]

Understandably, international public opinion worries about this new Italian political experiment, even if it often treats it as yet another example of political buffoonery and ordinary corruption. Political scientists and political commentators have focused on the most appalling aspects of Berlusconi's regime, such as the laws that his cabinets have passed to shield him from the judiciary; his determination to preserve political corruption (his long-term partner Cesare Previti has been found guilty of bribery and sentenced to six years of imprisonment); his alleged connections with organized crime (his other partner in business and politics, Marcello Dell'Utri, has been sentenced to eight years of imprisonment for his ties with the Sicilian Mafia); his open contempt for the judiciary and the Constitutional Court (he regards both as unacceptable limitations of his power based on the people's consent); the various sex scandals that have prompted some commentators to coin the expressions "bordello state" and "whoreocracy"; and his strong friendship with political leaders of impeccable democratic credentials such as Putin and Gaddafi.[2]

The purpose of this study is to better understand this new, ambiguous, protean type of political power that was born not against but within democratic institutions. Some scholars have suggested the analogy with Fascism; others with despotism, a kind of "sultanate"; others still maintain that it is just a version of populism, a degeneration of democracy into the power of a demagogue capable of persuading a corrupt demos.

I think that these interpretations do not properly describe Berlusconi's political creation. The analogy with Fascism holds only to a small extent. Fascism seized power (thanks to the Savoy monarchy's irresponsibility) through the systematic use of violence, including the assassination of political opponents (Giacomo Matteotti, Piero Gobetti, Giovanni Amendola, to cite only a few names), and kept it through the demolition of civil liberties. Berlusconi has surely used various forms of pressures against his opponents but never commissioned assassinations nor has put anyone in jail for political reasons. Political liberty and civil rights are in Italy still in place, even if Berlusconi's methods can be questioned on the grounds of constitutional legitimacy.[3] Newspapers and televisions (those not owned or controlled by Berlusconi) can print or broadcast harsh criticism against the government, citizens can freely organize rallies, and the opposition can raise its voice in the Parliament. In addition, Fascist ideology was nationalistic, heroic, and pervaded by an exalted longing for greatness. Nothing of that sort is to be found in Berlusconi's practice and language.

The concept of despotism too, the "sultanate," has a polemic value but does not capture the core of Berlusconi's regime.[4] The sultanate evokes an exotic and distant regime sustained by tradition. This is not Berlusconi's case. He would surely like to be considered as a sultan (and many of his supporters regard him in this way), but he is as indigenous as one can be and lacks the aura of tradition, not to mention the absence of an explicit support of religion, even if the Vatican has in many occasions helped him in spite of his questionable moral behavior.

Berlusconi's regime is surely a degeneration of democracy into the power of a demagogue who controls a corrupt demos properly tamed by his media. Like classic demagogues, Berlusconi has displayed since the beginning of his political career a remarkable ability to fascinate the demos with theatrical techniques designed to exalt his image as well as an equally impressive ability to obtain the demos' consent by telling them exactly what they want to hear. All his speeches are skillfully crafted in order to exploit the demos' beliefs and offer a comforting and simplified vision of reality.

Unlike almost all demagogues, however, Berlusconi is immensely rich, and he uses his fortune to obtain and consolidate political power. With his money he buys people, as we have seen during the political turmoil that has invested his government between the end of 2010 and the early months of 2011, when his parliamentary majority was about to dissolve. In more ordinary circumstances he uses his money to distribute favor of various sorts and value, from presents to jobs. In turn, he gets, as it has always been the case with this sort of politics, the loyalty of a large number of supporters. One would be therefore tempted to say that Berlusconi has established an oligarchy within a democratic system.

In addition, Berlusconi's regime has some traits that classical political philosophers have described as typical of tyranny. I mean here tyranny not in the sense of a power imposed and maintained through violence, but in the sense of a "veiled tyranny." Interestingly, this concept was, to my knowledge, first expounded in Italy by the fourteenth-century jurist Bartolus da Sassoferrato. The "veiled tyranny" is a political regime that has not established itself illegally, nor needs to resort to the use of massive coercion and can effectively attain its goals under the shadow of republican or democratic institutions. The best historical example was, as I explain in this book, the Medici's regime in Florence. Yet, like any tyranny, it is a use of power by a man for his own interest against the common good. Berlusconi's mentality can be defined as tyrannical, as Norberto Bobbio has claimed. He believes himself to be omnipotent and to be allowed to do what normal mortals can only dream of, including possessing all women, the younger the better.[5]

By examining Berlusconi's regime through the lens of classical political thought, we can conclude that it is a combination of the three forms of corrupt government: demagoguery, tyranny, and oligarchy.[6] It is a remarkable example of Italian political creativity, and yet another piece of evidence of a distinctive feature of Italian political history, namely, the failure to preserve liberty. Free city-republics of the late Middle Age did not succeed in defending themselves from internal corruption or foreign domination and all became open or veiled tyrannies; the liberal regime established by the Risorgimento in 1861 was dismantled fifty years later by Fascism; the democratic republic born on June 2, 1946, on the ashes of Fascism, has degenerated into Berlusconi's system. A country of fragile liberty, this is Italy's distinctive feature.

As I contend in this book, the mere existence of Berlusconi's enormous power—regardless of how he uses it—has made Italians unfree, or better, free, but in the sense of the liberty of the servants, not of the liberty of the citizens. My argument is based on the classical republican concept of political liberty that teaches us that the freedom of the citizen does not consist in being allowed to do more or less what we want but in being free from domination—that is, not to be subject to the arbitrary or enormous power of a man or some men. If a man has an enormous power he can easily impose his will against the common good and force citizens to follow his will, thereby reducing them to a condition of servitude. In addition, a man with an enormous or arbitrary power creates around and under him a court composed of a more or less large number of individuals who depend on him to obtain favors, power, and fame. Even if Berlusconi's regime surely is a lethal mixture of demagoguery, oligarchy, and veiled tyranny, its proper name is therefore the court system, and he is a new signore, a term which will be explained in Chapter 2 of this book.

With the court, as I document in this study, come the habits of servility: flattery, simulation, obsession with appearances, and complete identification with the feelings, the thoughts, and the will of the signore, not to mention the presence of women ready to offer their services and to magnify his splendor. Unlike early-modern and modern princely and imperial courts that affected some hundreds or thousands of individuals, Berlusconi's court system influences practically the whole country through the power of media. A servile mentality and corruption reach even the most remote areas of Italian social life. While authoritarian regimes control bodies, the new court system governs the minds, and it has thereby created a new type of human being. Incredible as it might appear, it has been able to produce an anthropological transformation on a large scale. Nothing comparable, to my knowledge, has ever being achieved in political history. One can stretch as much as we want the concept of liberty, but servile mentality has always been and remains incompatible with a free way of life.

Why are we Italians inept at preserving liberty? We suffer, as I argue in this essay, of a moral malaise that has been affecting us for centuries. With the exception of small elites that have dignified our history, we lack the sense of moral liberty, as Carlo Rosselli powerfully wrote about in *Liberal Socialism*, (1928–29): "It is a sad thing but true, that the education of man in Italy, the formation of the basic moral cell— i.e., the individual—is in large part still to be done. Most people lack the jealous and profound sense of autonomy and responsibility, because of misery, indifference, secular renunciation. Centuries of serfdom got the average Italian to oscillate between servile habit and anarchic revolt. He lacks the concept of life as struggle and mission, the notion of liberty as moral duty, the awareness of his own and the other's limits." Berlusconi is surely unfit to govern a democratic republic, but we Italians, we must face it, are unfit for liberty.

In the specific case of Berlusconi's ascent to power, however, there is also a visible and serious responsibility of the political and intellectual elite. Political judgments must be based on deeds, and the fact is that these elites have failed to prevent the formation of the enormous power of Silvio Berlusconi and have not yet been able to defeat it. Is their failure attributable to lack of wisdom or lack of moral integrity? Have they failed because they have not understood, or because they lack the moral distance needed to fight the new *signore* with intransigence? Whatever the answer, the point is that a significant part of the current political elite that opposes Berlusconi, with various degrees of consistency and determination, has failed. A new one must come forth if Italians want to entertain some hope for a civic rebirth.

The last chapter of the book, entitled "The Path to Freedom," attempts to indicate a possible way out of servitude in a sustained effort of civic education designed to form a new and different political leadership guided and inspired by a sincere devotion to the civic duties that the Constitution indicates. Berlusconi's ultimate goal is to dismantle the republican Constitution to give his domination a stronger institutional basis. He wants to reduce the power of all the institutions—the presidency of the republic, the Constitutional Court, the independency of the judiciary—that somehow still limit his domination. The emancipation from the liberty of the servants must on the contrary take the Constitution as its guiding principle.

International public opinion might think that Berlusconi is just an Italian extravagance. Improbable as it might appear, however, Berlusconi's methods and language could find imitators in other countries. No democratic polity is immune to the combined power of media and money. The media persuade and seduce the demos; money buys consent and loyalty. In political matters caution is preferable to excessive self-confidence. Citizens of democratic countries should therefore learn from Italy's mistakes and prepare ahead of time the appropriate defenses against the rise of enormous power. It is in this spirit that I am presenting this book to English-speaking readers.

THE LIBERTY OF SERVANTS

1

THE LIBERTY OF SERVANTS
AND THE LIBERTY OF CITIZENS

Italy is a free country, if by free we mean that neither other individuals nor the state can prevent us from doing as we choose. Everyone can do the things they want, provided that they have the resources and the ability: they can live where they like, express their own opinions, associate freely, vote for one candidate or another, criticize those who govern them, educate their children as they think best, profess this or that religion or profess no religion at all.

You might persuasively argue that actually many Italians cannot attain goals that they would like to pursue: they are unable to live in security, to enjoy an education worthy of the name, to avail themselves of adequate health care or minimal social services, leaving aside the fact that access to public honors and careers is governed by ironbound laws of patronage and that vast swaths of the national territory are under the control of organized crime. Still, the stumbling blocks that prevent many from achieving their goals are the result of misgovernment or corruption or inequality, not coercion imposed by force, with the exception of organized crime and the Mafia. If we can rightly point to violations of liberty only in cases where fundamental civil and political rights are suppressed by force, then we Italians are, generally speaking, a free people.

We can turn to the opinion of respected philosophers to find support for the idea that a country in which citizens can freely exercise and enjoy political and civil rights is a free country. Benjamin Constant, for instance, in his *The Liberty of Ancients Compared with that of Moderns*, makes a distinction between the liberty of ancient peoples—which "consisted in exercising collectively, but directly, several parts of the complete sovereignty; in deliberating, in the public square, over war and peace; in forming alliances with foreign governments; in voting laws, in pronouncing judgments; in examining the accounts, the acts, the stewardship of the magistrates; in calling them to appear in front of the assembled people, in accusing, condemning or absolving them"—and the liberty of modern peoples, which consists in "the right to be subjected only to the laws, and to be neither arrested, detained, put to death or maltreated in any way by the arbitrary will of one or more individuals," in "the right of everyone to express their opinion, choose a profession and practice it, to dispose of property, and even to abuse it; to come and go without permission, and without having to account for their motives or undertakings," in "everyone's right to associate with other individuals, either to discuss their interests, or to profess the religion which they and their associates prefer, or even simply to occupy their days or hours in a way which is most compatible with their inclinations or whims," and lastly, in everyone's right "to exercise some influence on the administration of the government, either by electing all or particular officials, or through representations, petitions, demands to which the authorities are more or less compelled to pay heed."[1]

More than a century after Benjamin Constant wrote those words, the philosopher Isaiah Berlin, in his essay "Two Concepts of Liberty" (1958), explains that true liberty consists of the fact that no man or group of men interferes with my activities and coincides with the area within which "a man can act unobstructed by others."[2] There also exists another idea of liberty, positive liberty, which springs from the desire to be masters of ourselves and to take part in the shaping of the laws and regulations that govern our lives. Although such a desire is legitimate, Berlin warns us, the ideal of positive liberty has historically been a disguise for tyranny. Therefore, true liberty is negative liberty. In more recent years, Fernando Savater has summarized in the following words the most common understanding of the word *liberty*, the definition most frequently utilized in everyday conversations and in political discussions: "[The word *liberty*] refers to a situation in which there are no physical, psychological or legal impediments that prevent us from acting in the way we wish to act. In this sense, a person who is not tied up, imprisoned, or in some way paralysed is free to move, to come and go; a person who is not subject to threats, tortured or drugged is free to speak or remain silent, to tell the truth or lie; a person who is not excluded or marginalized by discriminatory laws or does not suffer under extreme poverty or extreme ignorance is free to participate in public life and run for office."[3]

The problem is that liberty, if understood as an absence of impediments, is not in and of itself the liberty of citizens. Instead it can be the liberty of servants and subjects. The clearest possible statement of this idea can be found in the words of the political philosopher who first described it, Thomas Hobbes, in chapter 21 of *Leviathan* (1651): "Liberty, or freedom, signifieth properly the absence of opposition," and therefore "a freeman is he that, in those things which by his strength and wit he is able to do, is not hindered to do what he has a will to." To dispel any potential doubt, Hobbes goes on to tell us that such liberty is "consistent with the unlimited power of the sovereign."[4] The same warning is repeated by Isaiah Berlin, for that matter, when he notes that liberty understood as an absence of impediments can also be the liberty of servants or subjects conceded by an absolute sovereign.[5]

If the masters or the sovereigns are good, or weak, or foolish, or they have no interest in oppressing them, the servants and the subjects can enjoy the freedom to do more or less as they please. Classical comedies feature many examples of slaves or servants who are happy because no one is hindering or oppressing them. The servant Tranio in Plautus's *Mostellaria* can satisfy any whim he may have, as Grumio, a less-fortunate country slave, resentfully points out: "While you choose to, and have the opportunity, drink on, squander his property, corrupt my master's son, a most worthy young man, drink night and day, live like Greeks, make purchase of mistresses, give them their freedom, feed parasites, feast yourselves sumptuously. Was it thus that the old gentleman enjoined you when he went hence abroad? Is it after this fashion that he will find his property well husbanded? Do you suppose that this is the duty of a good servant, to be ruining both the estate and the son of his master?" His condition is actually enviable: "What would you have to be done?" laments poor Grumio. "It isn't all that can smell of foreign perfumes, if you smell of them; or that can take their places at table above their master, or live on such exquisite dainties as you live upon. Do you keep to yourself those turtle-doves, that fish, and poultry; let me enjoy my lot upon garlick diet. You are fortunate; I unlucky. It must be endured." Tranio is perfectly well aware of his good fortune, and he does not perceive servitude as a burden at all: "You seem, Grumio, as though you envied me, because I enjoy myself and you are wretched. It is quite my due. It's proper for me to make love, and for you to feed the cattle; for me to fare handsomely, you in a miserable way."[6]

Truffaldino, to cite one modern example, is even the servant of two masters and does whatever he likes: he eats, he drinks, and he earns money. He bemoans his state when he feels that his masters are not good to him: "When they say we ought to serve our masters with love, they ought to tell the masters to have a little charity toward their servants."[7] It happens sometimes that he is beaten, but that's not a huge problem, considering his advantages: "I don't care that for my beating! I have eaten well, I've dined well, and this evening I shall sup still better; and as long as I can serve two masters, there's this at least, that I draw double wages."[8] Serving two masters may be behavior that is less than entirely honest, but in the final analysis, it's excusable: "Yes sir, I did, that was the very trick. I took on the job without thinking; just to see what I could do. It did not last long, 'tis true; but at any rate I can boast that nobody would ever have found me out, if I had not given myself away for love of this girl here. I have done a hard day's work, and I dare say I had my shortcomings, but I hope that in consideration of the fun of the thing, all these ladies and gentlemen will forgive me."[9]

The liberty of citizens, or republican liberty, is quite another matter. It does not consist of not being hindered, or in merely not being oppressed, but rather of not being dominated, which is to say, not being subjected to the arbitrary or enormous power of another man or other men. By arbitrary power I mean the power of someone who can impose his will when and as he pleases, with no restriction by other powers. An enormous power is a power that is far superior to that of other citizens, so powerful that it can sidestep the sanctions of law or do with them as it pleases. According to the current understanding of such matters, our liberty can only be suffocated by the actions of other men; according to the republican conception, the liberty of the citizen dies because of the mere existence of an arbitrary or enormous power.

Even if the arbitrary or enormous power has established itself through legitimate methods and operates on behalf of its subjects or servants, its very existence makes the citizens servants.

Even though I have previously written about this topic, it is useful to clearly outline the concept of dependency and the difference between dependency and interference. In order to do so, let me make use of a few examples: a tyrant or an oligarchy that can oppress without fear of incurring the sanctions established by law; a wife who can be mistreated by her husband without being able either to resist or obtain reparation; workers who can be subjected to all sorts of abuse, both trivial and grave, by their employer or by a superior; the retirees who must rely on the whims of an official in order to receive a pension that is legitimately due to them; sick people who are obliged to rely on the willingness of a physician to receive treatment; young scholars who know that their careers depend not on the excellence of their work but on the caprices of their professor; citizens who can be tossed into prison arbitrarily by the police. In none of the cases that I have just described is there any interference: I did not describe a tyrant or an oligarchy that oppress; rather, they *can* oppress, if they so choose; I didn't say that the husband mistreated his wife, only that he *can* mistreat her without fear of retribution from the law. The same thing is true of the employer, the doctor, the professor, the official, and the policemen that I mentioned. None of them prevents anyone from pursuing the ends that they wish to pursue; no one is interfering with anyone else's life. The subjects—the wife, the workers, the elderly, the retirees, and the young scholars—are all completely free, if by liberty we mean not being hindered or constrained. But they are, at the same time, in a condition of dependency, and therefore servants, if we reason in accordance with the principle of the liberty of the citizen.

Let me add that the concept of liberty as the absence of dependency on an arbitrary or enormous power is based not on an evaluation of intentions, but rather a realistic observation. Whether the intentions of those who possess arbitrary or enormous power are good or evil is entirely irrelevant. The problem is that those who have arbitrary or enormous power can easily impose their own interest and that this power engenders a servile mentality in those who are subject to it, with all the retinue of qualities and actions such as adulation, vicious gossip, inability to judge clearly, identification with the words and actions of the signore, scorn for the generous and great hearted, cynicism, indifference, simulation, abuse of the weak and bullying of one's adversaries, lack of an inner life, and obsession with appearances. These ways of thinking and living are incompatible with liberty because liberty demands that citizens be unwilling either to serve humbly or dominate arrogantly.[10]

The idea that being free means not being subject to enormous or arbitrary powers has been upheld by many authoritative political writers of antiquity and modern times. Cicero, after clearly stating that true liberty exists "only in that republic in which the people has the highest power" and where there is "an absolute equality of rights," summarizes in just a few words the essence of the concept: "liberty... does consist in having a good master, but in having no master at all."[11] This conception was borrowed and developed by the Italian jurists and political philosophers of the Humanist period. With few exceptions, they insist on the idea that the essential element of political liberty is independence from the arbitrary power of a man. For that reason, they identify the liberty of a city with its power to endow itself with statutes and laws. In contrast, they consider a city to be in servitude that had received statutes and laws from the emperor or which was obliged to ask for the emperor's approval. The source that the jurists cite for their interpretation of political liberty as an absence of personal dependency is Roman law, and in particular those passages in which a free person is defined as a person not subject to the dominion (*dominium*) of another. The opposite of the free condition is the servile condition, which is to say the condition of an individual who depends on the will of another.[12] Following in the path of the same tradition, Machiavelli explains the concept of liberty of the citizen with such clarity that no comment whatever is required: "free men" are those who are not "depending on others,"[13] while the status of the citizen is the opposite of that of the slave: "born free and not slaves."[14]

This concept of liberty has been defended both by liberal political authors and by their republican counterparts. Suffice it to quote from two examples, John Locke and Jean-Jacques Rousseau. Locke states that the true liberty of an individual is "to dispose and order freely as he lists his person, actions, possessions, and his whole property within the allowance of those laws under which he is, and therein not to be subject to the arbitrary will of another, but freely follow his own."[15] Rousseau writes that "a free people obeys, but it does not serve, it has leaders but no masters; it obeys the laws, but it obeys only the laws, and it is due to the strength of the laws that it is not forced to obey men."[16] If we study the sources of republican and liberal political thought, both ancient and modern, the answer to the question—"what is the liberty of the citizen?"— is always the same: to be free does not so much mean not being hindered or oppressed as much as it means not being dependent on a man or certain men who have an arbitrary or enormous power over us. The lack of liberty then is not only the consequence of actions that we undergo against our will, but it can also be a simple condition. To put it very concisely: if we are subjected to the arbitrary or enormous power of a man, we may well be free to do more or less what we want, but we are still servants.

Before we move away from history and begin examining the present day, it is indispensable for us to explore two fundamental aspects of the liberty of citizens, first and foremost the relationship between liberty and the law. According to the ideas that dominate in our times, liberty is greater, the fewer in number and the weaker the laws that limit our possibilities of action. Here too the political thinker we should cite is the one who more than anyone else detested the liberty of the citizen, Thomas Hobbes. In fact, he explains that laws are like "artificial chains" that are fastened to the lips of the sovereign and terminate in the ears of the subjects as well as binding their hands. Let us abandon the metaphor: laws bind, impede, and hinder and therefore the "liberty of a subject" consists, properly speaking, only in those actions that the sovereign has neglected to discipline by means of civil laws. The smaller the area of activity that is regulated by laws, the greater the liberty of the subjects.[17]

In contrast, the liberty of citizens is not a liberty *from* laws, but a liberty *through* or *in virtue* of laws. In order for there to be true liberty it is necessary for everyone to be subject to the laws or, in the words of the classical precept, that laws be more powerful than men. If, in a state, instead there is a man who is more powerful than the laws then there exists no liberty for the citizens. In fifteenth-century Florence, without any open and systematic use of violence, the Medici established an enormous power, so great that they were able to violate or dominate the laws and therefore made the city their servant. That is why we read in the *Ricordi* of Filippo Rinuccini, an opponent of the Medici, that a republic that wishes to "live in liberty" should not allow a citizen "to be more powerful than the laws."[18] About Piero de' Medici, the son of Cosimo the Elder, Rinuccini wrote: "So it was clearly visible that he was manifestly a tyrant in our city; for this is what happens when one is allowed to become too much greater over all the others, which is something that is deeply pernicious in a republic, and always leads to this outcome."[19] Machiavelli echoes him in the *Discourses on the First Ten Books of Titus Livy*: "That a city could not call itself free where there was a citizen who was feared by the magistrates."[20]

The contrast between the liberty of subjects (liberty *from* laws) and the liberty of citizens (liberty *through* laws) becomes clear when we read an amusing passage from *Leviathan* in which Hobbes is attempting to persuade us that there is actually no difference between the two liberties, and that the citizen of a republic where the rule of law prevails is just as free as the subject of the most absolute of sovereigns: "There is written on the turrets of the city of Luca in great characters at this day, the word LIBERTAS; yet no man can thence infer that a particular man has more liberty or immunity from the service of the Commonwealth there than in Constantinople. Whether a Commonwealth be monarchical or popular [republican], the freedom is still the same."[21]

What Hobbes fails to understand, or pretends not to understand, is that in a (noncorrupt) republic both the governors and the governed are subject to civil and constitutional laws, while in Constantinople the sultan is above the law and is free to dispose arbitrarily of the property and the lives of his subjects, thus obliging them to live in a condition of dependency, and therefore without liberty. In spite of all of Hobbes's dialectical efforts, the liberty of citizens and the liberty of subjects and servants are profoundly different.

That the liberty of citizens and the liberty of subjects inspire ways of thinking and living that are impossible to reconcile is unmistakable if we consider the relationship between liberty and virtue. In current opinion, liberty is a possession that we hold and that we can enjoy at our pleasure. We do not need to live in one manner rather than another or do something particular *in order* to be free. The liberty of the citizen, in contrast, is not a possession that one has and one enjoys, however we may live, but the reward that we receive if we do good, or if we perform our civil duties.

The reason that liberty is not a possession that can be enjoyed but a reward for duties performed is easy to understand if we look at the realities of life. In every population and throughout history (to a lesser or greater degree) there have been and there are men who like to dominate other men, climb ever higher, and be always at the center of things. To attain their objective, they accumulate and consolidate great powers in many different ways. If we wish to prevent a single man from establishing his dominion over the polity, it is necessary for the citizens, or at least the wiser ones, to perceive the danger before it is too late and be able to identify the best ways to defend the common good. They must also show that they possess virtues, to use an old but still appropriate term, and in particular prudence and courage. If, due to their stupidity or cowardice, they fail to oppose the powerful men who wish to dominate them, they will lose their liberty. For a subject or a servant, to be free means only to have liberty and enjoy it without interference or hindrance; for citizens it is the reward for having acted in accordance with virtue.

2

THE COURT SYSTEM

If being free citizens means not being subjected to an enormous power and performing one's civil duties, it is evident that the Italians cannot claim to be free; that is to say, they may be free, but only free in the sense of the liberty of servants. In Italy, in fact, a power has established itself that is neither arbitrary, nor authoritarian, nor despotic, nor illegitimate, but it is enormous and by its very existence it destroys the liberty of the citizens. The power of Silvio Berlusconi is not arbitrary, because it is not sufficiently great to impose its own will arbitrarily; it is not authoritarian, because it was not established and it does not endure through the deployment of police violence or private armed forces; it is legitimate, because it is based on the consent of the majority of the Italians, expressed in compliance with the rules of democracy. It is nonetheless an enormous power in the strict sense of the term, inasmuch as it grossly exceeds the limits of power that any other man has ever had in a liberal or democratic regime. Silvio Berlusconi possesses a personal wealth that no democratic political leader has ever even remotely dreamed of possessing; he controls a political party that he himself founded, made up of people faithful not to an ideal, but to him personally; he controls a system of mass communications that no head of government has ever had available to him.

It certainly doesn't require a lot of words to make it clear that money is not a private issue but a genuine source of political power. Money makes it possible to distribute favors, that is, benefits that are not endowed for particular reasons or merits, but only because the oligarch believes that the person thus benefited will recompense him with "friendship," loyalty, and even devotion. Those who obtain favors and who know that they owe them to a powerful person and not to their own merits will immediately lose the mentality of a free person, if they ever possessed it, and will become a supporter of that powerful person, both in hope of new favors and in order to avoid the loss of those they now possess. Enormous wealth can thus easily be transformed into a vast network of electoral consensus.[1] To control a party made up of devoted people means being in a position to conquer votes and, with those votes, access to political power. Running a media empire means being capable of persuading millions of people.[2] At the risk of repeating myself: it does not matter who possesses such power; it is also irrelevant whether he uses it well or badly. The mere fact that a power of such scope and characteristics should exist automatically transforms the citizens into servants.

When an enormous or arbitrary power establishes itself in a country, the court system is born. A court exists when a person, by virtue of his enormous power, constantly occupies a more elevated and central position in relation to a relatively large number of individuals who depend on him in order to gain, keep, and increase their wealth, status, and chance of appearing and being seen and admired. This system depends on the effective power of the signore—I use this term to identify whoever occupies on an ongoing basis the superior and central position—to distribute to the courtiers material and symbolic benefits and to threaten them, equally effectively, with the loss of those goods. In the court system, the prince too depends to a certain degree on the courtiers and all those whom he can benefit or threaten. But the superior power of the signore and his central position are not in question. The members of a court, Norbert Elias writes, "were all more or less dependent on the king. The smallest nuance in his behavior towards them was therefore important to them; it was the visible indicator of their relation to him and their position within court society. But this dependence indirectly shaped the behavior of court people towards each other."[3]

The most important reason for a court's existence is the practice of servitude. Even Baldesar Castiglione, the most influential author on the subject, points out that the courtier must be "energetic and faithful to whomever he serves."[4] A few years later, another author provided an even better description of the nature of service a courtier provides: "Profit engenders love, thus those who serve, / And who profit by their servitude, / Are obliged to serve faithfully."[5] One may serve out of honor or debt or for any other reason, but serving is inevitably tantamount to courting and accompanying one's signore and doing one's best to join oneself as closely as possible to him. A compleat servant is one who abandons his soul and dons the soul of the signore in its place, and a court is a congregation of men assembled to pursue the same end of serving: "It happens that as soon as the master has spoken, the conscientious secretary will have penetrated with his mind the aim toward which his master tends." In short, the courtier must "garb himself in the master's emotions," and live in accordance with his reason.[6]

It's one thing to serve a signore, quite another, we should keep in mind, to serve the republic. Those who wrote about the court and courtiers knew that well. In the dialogue *Il Malpiglio: A Dialogue on the Court*, Torquato Tasso has the Neapolitan Stranger, the character who expresses his own ideas, say that since "republics and courts are not the same," a different kind of honor is sought in the former and the latter contexts. One of the participants observes that "in republics, a man both serves and rules. Men in the lower ranks obey their leaders, but sometimes the positions are reversed. Then those who used to rule their equals obey, and those who once obeyed rule. And even those who have reached the highest offices are like servants of the laws." Thus, comments the Neapolitan Stranger, servitude in a republic is different from servitude in a court: "In spite of appearances, we prefer to call this one freedom; and we call what I was describing servitude, although in many ways it reveals the greatness of princely rule."[7]

However different courtiers may be one from another and however hostile they may be to one another, the court is a mass and as such it has the power to irradiate its own behaviors to the most distant corners of the nation. The court diffuses itself throughout the country, like a spider at the center of its web. If it moves, everything moves.[8] The behavior of courtiers, writes Elias Canetti, "infects, and is intended to infect, the ruler's other subjects" and "what the courtier does all the time, they should be at pains to do periodically." The men that form the court "all have their own separate functions and, to each other, seem to be quite different. But to the rest of the world they—the courtiers—appear as identical parts of a single unit, radiating the loyalty they have in common."[9] The prince and the courtiers are models to be imitated. "The life of the prince," Castiglione reminds us once again, "is a norm and guide for the citizens, and all behavior must needs depend on his behavior."[10]

The court is a theater of courtesy and entertainment.[11] Historically, the court flourished and experienced its moments of greatest splendor in the principalities, the monarchies, and the empires, where the prince, the king, or the emperor are elevated above the others and placed at the center by acknowledged and sanctioned right. All the same, there are examples of court systems in a republican regime as well, or at least in the shadows of republican institutions and constitutions. The best-known court system is the one that the Medici constructed in Florence beginning in 1512. Having been restored to their rule over the city with the decisive reinforcement of soldiers provided by the pope, and having conquered an enormous power with the threat of armed might, the descendants of Cosimo the Elder and Lorenzo the Magnificent introduced reforms that substantially modified the political power structure while preserving, at least in appearance, the republican institutions. But Florence, despite the institutional changes, remained a republic. The Medici were only citizens who held much greater power than anyone else as a result of their wealth and their international connections, in particular with the papal court of Rome. The true change, however, came in terms of mores. The republic required citizens; the Medici regime wanted courtiers and set about rooting out from the minds and hearts of the Florentine people the ways of civil living and training them up to court living.

It was Machiavelli who had understood how a court system can operate in the shadows of republican institutions, where he explains that there are two ways of obtaining power in a republic, public modes and private ways. The public modes are "when one individual by counseling well, by working better in the common benefit, acquires reputation"; the private ways, are, in contrast, "doing benefit to this and to that other private individual—by lending him money, marrying his daughters for him, defending him from the magistrates, and doing him similar private favors that make men partisans to oneself and give spirit to whoever is so favored to be able to corrupt the public and to breach the laws." "A well-ordered republic ought, therefore," Machiavelli concludes, to open its doors "to whoever seeks support through public ways, and close them to whoever seeks it through private ways."[12]

In the court system, violence, or the threat of violence, to bodies or property, plays only a marginal role. Because there is no violence, there is no oppression: no one is coerced into doing what they do not choose to do; no one is prevented from doing what they want and are able to do. Everyone is free; and yet there is a man who is above and at the center of a congregation of individuals who serve his will. It is no different from the voluntary servitude described by Etienne de La Boétie:

> I come now to a point which is, in my opinion, the mainspring and the secret of domination, the support and foundation of tyranny. Whoever thinks that halberds, sentries, the placing of the watch, serve to protect and shield tyrants is, in my judgment, completely mistaken. These are used, it seems to me, more for ceremony and a show of force than for any reliance placed in them. The archers forbid the entrance to the palace to the poorly dressed who have no weapons, not to the well armed who can carry out some plot. Certainly it is easy to say of the Roman emperors that fewer escaped from danger by the aid of their guards than were killed by their own archers. It is not the troops on horseback, it is not the companies afoot, it is not arms that defend the tyrant. This does not seem credible on first thought, but it is nevertheless true that there are only

four or five who maintain the dictator, four or five who keep the country in bondage to him. Five or six have always had access to his ear, and have either gone to him of their own accord, or else have been summoned by him, to be accomplices in his cruelties, companions in his pleasures, panders to his lusts, and sharers in his plunders. These six manage their chief so successfully that he comes to be held accountable not only for his own misdeeds but even for theirs. The six have six hundred who profit under them, and with the six hundred they do what they have accomplished with their tyrant. The six hundred maintain under them six thousand, whom they promote in rank, upon whom they confer the government of provinces or the direction of finances, in order that they may serve as instruments of avarice and cruelty, executing orders at the proper time and working such havoc all around that they could not last except under the shadow of the six hundred, nor be exempt from law and punishment except through their influence. The consequence of all this is fatal indeed. And whoever is pleased to unwind the skein will observe that not the six thousand but a hundred thousand, and even millions, cling to the tyrant by this cord to which they are tied.... In short, when the point is reached, through big favors or little ones, that large profits or small are obtained under a tyrant, there are found almost as many people to whom tyranny seems advantageous as those to whom liberty would seem desirable.[13]

The liberty of servants is a precarious liberty. All that is required is a shift in mood or determination on the part of the prince and the servant will find himself in the blink of an eye deprived of his privileges and expelled, or expelled once again, into the shadows. Not only is this liberty precarious, it is also difficult to conquer and even more difficult to preserve. It brings riches, but through the favor of the prince, not through hard work or brilliance; it shines a splendid light, but that light is reflected. Both the riches and the splendor are paid for with anxieties, worries, and fears. Under the appearance of a life of triumph, the courtier is actually unhappy: "For, in all honesty, can it be in any way except in folly that you approach a tyrant, withdrawing further from your liberty and, so to speak, embracing with both hands your servitude? Let such men lay aside briefly their ambition, or let them forget for a moment their avarice, and look at themselves as they really are. Then they will realize clearly that the townspeople, the peasants whom they trample under foot and treat worse than convicts or slaves, they will realize, I say, that these people, mistreated as they may be, are nevertheless, in comparison with themselves, better off and fairly free."[14]

The oppressed are free; the courtiers are servants. In this apparently absurd statement we find the secret of the liberty of servants. Those who are subjected to the oppression of the court system find that they have been denied the benefits to which they would have a right, or else subjected to burdens that they have no obligation to take on. They must submit, but no one asks them to focus all their thoughts and all their will to please the man who dominates them. Those who are part of the court system must instead renounce their own selves:

> The tiller of the soil and the artisan, no matter how enslaved, discharge their obligation when they do what they are told to do; but the dictator sees men about him wooing and begging his favor, and doing much more than he tells them to do. Such men must not only obey orders; they must anticipate his wishes; to satisfy him they must foresee his desires; they must wear themselves out, torment themselves, kill themselves with work in his interest, and accept his pleasure as their own, neglecting their preferences for his, distorting their character and corrupting their nature; they must pay heed to his words, to his intonation, to his gestures, and to his glance. Let them have no eye, nor foot, nor hand that is not alert to respond to his wishes or to seek out his thoughts.[15]

While oppression binds one's actions but leaves the will and the mind unfettered, dependency on another man and servitude that has been sought and desired both enter into one's will and thoughts. A servant who seeks his servitude, unlike a servant who is coerced by force, must learn to think,

speak, and act like his master. In short, he is obliged to identify with his master: "The meanings of the prince, which he
unfolds and reveals in his mind, become identified with him
to some extent: a mirror which reflects the best ideas of his
thoughts: And if his master speaks through his mouth and
writes through his hand, he cannot help but be the instrument of his grace, the declaration of his oracles." Like Pro-
teus, the courtier must transform himself into his signore,
interpret perfectly the impulses of his soul, actually clothe
himself in his affections.[16] Long and assiduous practice of the
art of identifying with one's master ensures that a voluntary
servant becomes a servant in his heart. His inner being emp-
ties itself and is entirely transferred into the external appearances of a behavior modeled on an imitation of the man on
whom he depends. Consumed as he is in thinking like his
master and desiring what his master wants, the voluntary
servant cannot even imagine that it is possible to have convictions of his own and a will to go with it. He therefore lacks
the distinctive mark of a free person, that is to say, a sense of
duty. He thoroughly knows his obligations (to perform them
or evade them); but he is excluded from the inner sense of
duty that springs from an inner quest.

A voluntary servant believes that he can no longer change
his own condition, and in many cases he does not even consider it desirable to do so. Being a servant, for various reasons, is the way he lives. He does not aspire to the liberty
of the citizen. He attributes his servitude to his own inepti-
tude, rather than to the cruelty of fate or of men. Truffaldino

states this explicitly: "Oh poor Truffaldin'! Rather than be a servant, devil take me, I'd—what indeed? By the grace of Heaven there's nothing I *can* do."[17] The character of the Doctor in *The Antiquarian's Family* laments his condition, but he is resigned: "Behold what fine honor one acquires by serving a high-born lady! For a little vanity, I'm obliged to suffer a hundred villainies. But I don't know what to do. I'm fond of it and I don't know how to break away."[18] Either because he does not feel that he is suited to living free, or else because his ambition leads him to accept servitude in expectation of honors and wealth, or else because he is simply accustomed to his condition, his mind and his will shut him up behind the invisible but tenacious bars of the liberty of servants.

Those who have written about the court system have underscored the ambivalent nature of the courtier's condition. The homage that courtiers pay to their signore "consists in *being there*, their faces turned toward the ruler, gathered round him, but not approaching him too close, dazzled by him, fearing him, and looking to him as the source of all things. In this unique atmosphere, in which splendor, terror and hope of favor are equally blended, they spend their lives. Nothing, or almost nothing, else exists for them. They have, as it were, colonized the sun; they show other men that it is habitable."[19]

Other authors have instead focused on the unhappiness that chills the life of the voluntary servant: "Can that be called a happy life? Can it be called living? Is there anything more intolerable than that situation, I won't say for a man of mettle nor even for a man of high birth, but simply for a man of common sense or, to go even further, for anyone having the face of a man? What condition is more wretched than to live thus, with nothing to call one's own, receiving from someone else one's sustenance, one's power to act, one's body, one's very life?"[20]

This opinion, expressed by La Boétie and many others, is deeply respectable. To the eyes of a person who has even the slightest sense of the worth of his own personal dignity, no servitude is as disagreeable as one that springs not from force but from dependency on the enormous power of another man. It is equally true though that it is a type of servitude that attracts many people. Alongside and perhaps even above and beyond the material advantages, the court offers fascinating possibilities of living life as if it were a part in a play in an immense theater under the eyes of the prince and of the millions who are outside and at the edges. "Whoever considers that the face of the prince constitutes the entire happiness of the courtier," we read in a treatise on courts, and that the courtier rejoices throughout his life "in seeing him and being seen," will quickly understand "how God can constitute all the glory and the happiness of the saints." In a court, the words *signoria* (seigniory) and *servitude* lose "much of their bitterness; and thus, like certain herbs left to soak in water, they have almost been macerated and softened by remaining in the mouths of men."[21]

Because of its ability to bestow benefits and to exert fascination, the court is quick to spring into existence and reinforce itself. In Italy it has been reborn and it has sunk roots in the shadow of republican institutions due to the effect of the enormous power of Silvio Berlusconi and the acquiescence of a substantial part of the political elite. His person is above and at the center of all the others who are operating in the political arena and of normal citizens. He does not depend on others who possess more power, while hundreds of thousands of people depend on him, directly or indirectly and, in order to preserve their benefits, they must work on his behalf. Silvio Berlusconi doesn't take orders, he gives them. He must accept limits to his own power, he has lost elections, and at times he must even make concessions to some of his more enterprising courtiers, but his superiority and his centrality are never called into question.

The same consideration can be applied to his centrality. Like the metaphor of superiority, the metaphor of centrality has no meaning in terms of value. It serves to describe the court system. From 1994 to the time of this writing (May 2010) all of Italy's political life has rotated around Silvio Berlusconi: all eyes turn to him, all thoughts, hopes, and fears. The courtiers who lived in princely and royal courts saw the prince or the king with their own eyes and listened to his words directly, but their number never exceeded a few thousand. Today, in the court that has sprung up inside a democracy, the populace of courtiers numbers millions of individuals, who thanks to the media of mass communication, see the prince and listen to his words every day. The centrality is constant. It has never been entirely eclipsed, and it has endured now for fifteen years, a span of time much longer than that of many courts of the past. This point was underscored not by an adversary of Berlusconi but one of his supporters: "In these last few days, Silvio Berlusconi has been celebrating his triumph. As I have already had an opportunity to point out, since the foundation of the Italian Republic no political leader has managed to achieve what he has achieved. As prime minister, Il Cavaliere, as he is known [Cavaliere is a title of honor bestowed by the President of the Italian Republic] has beaten every record for longevity, including those set by a long-distance runner of politics like Giulio Andreotti, who resided at Palazzo Chigi with his governments for more than six years."[22] Every organized society that has attained any degree of complexity has had a center occupied by a governing elite and a set of symbolic forms that express the presence and the power of that elite. The symbolic forms are visible signs of various sorts—images, rituals, processions, music, songs—by means of which the sovereign attracts all eyes to himself.[23] Whoever occupies the center, governs, judges, approves or disapproves, rewards or punishes, elevates or lowers both those who are close to the center and those who are far away. But aside from performing these actions, and often devoting more attention to it than he does to these actions, he will devote great energy to appearing, showing himself, performing, and fascinating others. "I say to you, Queen Elizabeth I of England said, that we princes are always on a stage."[24]

In the courts of premodern and modern history, the art of appearing and performing was governed by very exact rules, as Castiglione has illustrated. But the expressive activity of the center has not declined with the end of the princely court. It also lives and flourishes in the democracies of the present time. It matters little whether the members of the elite were more-or-less democratically selected, or whether or not they are profoundly split internally (and they often are divided to a much greater extent than an outside observer might suppose). "They justify their existence and order their actions in terms of a collection of stories, ceremonies, insignia, formalities, and appurtenances that they have either inherited or, in more revolutionary situations, invented. It is these—crowns and coronations, limousines and conferences—that mark the center as center and give what goes on there its aura of being not merely important but in some odd fashion connected with the way the world is built."[25]

Both the structure and the expressions of social life change, but their intimate necessity remains the same. Thrones and regal pomp and circumstance may go out of style, but political power still requires a cultural framework within which it can define itself and achieve its ends. A world that was completely demystified is a world that would be completely depoliticized. The dimension of the extraordinary has by no means vanished from the politics of the present day, even if a great deal of banality and a great deal of vulgarity has entered into it and continues to enter into it. Power continues to poison, but also to exalt. If we truly wish to understand a charismatic politician, even if we are dealing with a minor or ephemeral figure, we must focus our attention at the center. And in Italy, at the center, we find Silvio Berlusconi. The court system that he has built requires, by its very nature, a continuous series of performances and appearances. The signore, and with him the courtiers who are closest to him, must appear and act and inspire even those who are furthest away and who wish to enter the court or build another court. Therefore, political life becomes an immense theater or, as Filippo Ceccarelli has put it so adroitly, "a *teatrone*—a huge theater":

> It's nonsense to talk about the little theater of politics!
> If only. It's much bigger than that. It's a huge theater, if
> anything. A huge theater, by now. And there's no going
> back. In extreme and brutal synthesis: the spectacle has
> put checkmate to power and holds it prisoner, a pal-
> lid shadow of its former self, without even notifying
> it of its new condition of captivity. Nor do the rulers
> of the present day have the slightest wish to consider
> themselves under the domination of something that
> they themselves yearn after, strive for, and completely
> achieve, day after day, on the public stage.[26]

Silvio Berlusconi dominates the stage: he appears more than anyone else and plays the leading role among the costars, minor characters, and cameos. The other courtiers— however much they might agitate themselves, and talk, and shout, and complain—only glow to the extent that he allows them to appear and to place themselves in the spotlight. He never spares an effort to present himself in a captivating setting, usually with a background of fake skies and fluffy clouds. When the occasion demands it, he has full-fledged stage sets built, with shed-studios that are captivating in their unmistakable artificiality: "super-light, temporary structures, nicely organized and comfortable, but in particular designed to create a sense of wonderful astonishment in his guests and in the television audience. In short, places for spectacles, for shows."[27]

As the powerful have done throughout history, he changes places, transforms cities or builds new ones, and it matters little if they are papier-mâché and destined not to endure. For the G8 summit in Genoa, in July 2001, he demanded a city regulation that prohibited the citizens from hanging out laundry. He had billboards and advertising posters and television antennas removed to make everything look more orderly and antiseptic. He went so far as to camouflage the façade of an entire building, which he judged to be excessively modern, with a colossal mock-up worthy of the finest theater set, with fake colors, fake doors, fake windows, fake balconies, and a fake roof. Once the fake façade was in place, he issued a judgment that reveals his aesthetic vision: "I always say, fiction is better than reality." That fake city was his city, erected in his image and semblance, a visible sign of his greatness. He could stroll through the transmogrified streets and squares with the great and powerful of the planet in an enchanted universe marked by a red line. Outside was the real city, where his power showed in those days its brutal face of violence and bullying.

On another occasion, in Pratica di Mare, for the signing of the treaty between NATO and Russia, the signore did not limit himself to transforming reality, but instead constructed a new, entirely artificial reality, designed to attain the maximum optical effect. "Let's try to recreate a Roman atmosphere," he proclaimed. Money was no object, and entire nurseries and greenhouses were emptied to pretty up the airport with hedges, dwarf palm trees, and miles of sod strips. He had halls set up with statues of philosophers and jurists and with fiberglass reproductions of sculptures extending bouquets of flowers. In the Sala del Trattato he wanted the light blue of the heavens and the gold of the travertine. It was all fake, but who had ever done such a thing, before him?[28]

The Italian Parliament too is first and foremost a theater in which he can express his central and superior status. That is why he doesn't like being filmed by a static television camera that can only transmit, in his opinion, stiff and boring images. He is even less fond of the position afforded him in the Parliament as prime minister, too low in comparison with the location of the president of the Chamber of Deputies, who towers over him by a good five feet. To make matters worse, the president of the Chamber is given a solemn armchair and the use of a bell. On the occasion of a debate on a topic—conflicts of interest—that was of special concern to him, he tried unsuccessfully to have the set and the camera angles modified so that appearances would flatter him appropriately, highlighting his central role and his preeminence. In the republic of the spectacle, as Ceccarelli astutely points out, the supreme role no longer belongs to the Chamber of Deputies or the Senate, but to him.[29]

He's been called the "master and lord of the images." To appear and to perform are the means and the objective of his power. In both arts, he is unrivaled:

> No other politician, in fact, can come close to the variety of portrayals and performances of which Il Cavaliere is capable; he rehearses every part but also improvises, like any great actor. And he is one. With the same apparent naturalness, he can weep in the presence of the Ugandan children who are being treated at the Bambin Gesù Hospital and pull an alluring dance move when the Carabinieri band strikes up a spirited march. Onstage, he reacts instinctively, but he is extremely controlled; he pretends and is totally serious far better than many professionals. But unlike most actors, Berlusconi has vast amounts of money on his side, and perhaps too much power. He grabs symbols on the fly and plays with them with the rude vigor of a predator who has clawed his way to the summit of the public institutions, which are sacred as long as he's in charge of them. He knows how to make people love him, but he always wants to be at the center of attention, he expects and demands ovations, and he is never ashamed of anything or anyone.... He personally oversees the lighting, the colors, and the clouds of the backdrops. He always calculates the optimal distance between

himself and the audience and the elevation from which he should speak. He never wants anyone else behind him or above him.

A representation must always make it clear to those who see him that he is the center and that his power is much greater than that of all the others, including the institutions of the state.[30]

The sovereign, as medieval and modern philosophers and jurists inform us, has two bodies—one is physical and the other is mystical. The physical body is visible and mortal; the mystical body is invisible and immortal. Precisely because it is visible, the physical body must express the characteristics proper to sovereignty: perfection, splendor, strength. That is why sovereigns have always dedicated enormous care to their physical appearance and adorned their own bodies with carefully selected symbols and clothing. The signore of the Italian court imitates them. He devotes continuous care to his face to ensure that it is always free of imperfections and conveys the idea that he is capable of conquering time. Just as he is able to defeat time, the signore is also able to defeat death. He announces that he has suffered a serious illness only when he can proclaim that he has been able to triumph over the disease. His closest collaborators must likewise have fit and healthy bodies and show that they know how to triumph with their wills over the marks of decay and deterioration. Every Italian remembers the photographs taken in Bermuda of Berlusconi in a T-shirt and white shorts leading a platoon of his faithful followers as they jog and do calisthenics. It is the image of a ritual that expresses a hierarchical order and a determination to achieve physical asceticism in which the body is a medium of representation.

When he moves from place to place, the sovereign must arouse amazement and admiration. In centuries past, he obtained that objective through the magnificence of his horses, his carriages, his canopies, and the procession formed by the dignitaries and the soldiers who preceded him and followed him. Nowadays the preeminence and the centrality of the sovereign are assured by the motorcade of automobiles and the deployment of security forces. From this point of view as well, the signore of the Italian court has managed to outclass all the examples of the past. His appearances before his followers are always preceded by anthems and music. In order to deal adequately with the logistics of an electoral campaign, he went so far as to refit a large luxury ocean liner, rechristening it *Azzurra*, with an onboard auditorium capable of seating as many as five thousand people. In every port where it docked, it offered the populace the spectacle of the greatness of the signore and of his court. The success, the chronicler informs us, was spectacular: "A cheering Naples welcomes *Azzurra*: a fleet of boats awaits the big liner in the Gulf of Naples and in the sky the 'airplanes of liberty' salute the Flagship of Forza Italia. In the face of the warm response of the Neapolitans, Berlusconi is moved: 'It's a touching spectacle. We will continue our cruise-crusade for liberty,' he declares, 'with the memory in our hearts of an unforgettable day.' The same warmth is on display in Catania, Reggio Calabria, and Bari. The people of southern Italy celebrate and acclaim Berlusconi with spectacles of folkways, musical bands, and lots and lots of friendship. In the ports of Pescara, Ancona, Rimini, and Venice they await the arrival of *Azzurra*. Nearly one hundred thousand people have taken their seats in the huge auditorium."[31] One has the impression of reading the chronicle of the arrival of a prince or a pope. The democratic republic has changed in many ways in comparison with monarchies and principalities, but an enormous power still knows how to move people and capture their imaginations.

Machiavelli tells us that when the Medici were the *signori*—seigneurs, or lords—of Florence, one of the most unmistakable signs of their power (completely contrary to republican liberty) was their practice of debating political matters not in public halls, but in their own sumptuous palazzi. Don't we all know that Berlusconi has introduced the same practice? The places where a substantial portion of his political activity takes place are, in fact, Palazzo Grazioli in Rome, Villa San Martino in Arcore, Villa Certosa on the Costa Smeralda of Sardinia, and the Castello di Paraggi in Portofino. It is in these private spaces that he receives friends, members of Parliament, and heads of state. By so doing he tramples on the dignity and the majesty of Italy's public buildings and he exalts his own wealth and power. In his private residences, he presents himself with great splendor and eludes the gaze of public opinion. His power becomes alluring and secret, and therefore immense.

In every court there have always been courtesans: "Just as no court," Castiglione explains, "however great, can have adornment or splendor or gaiety in it without ladies, neither can any Courtier be graceful or pleasing or brave, or do any gallant deed of chivalry unless he is moved by the society and by the love and charm of ladies: even discussion about the Courtier is always imperfect unless ladies take part in it and add their part of that grace by which they make Courtiership perfect and adorned."[32] The role of women is to brighten the lives of the signore and the courtiers with their charms. Without them, the court would be grim and dull. Their number and their youth and beauty are both signs of the court's power. For their services, they are recompensed with various benefits, first and foremost the privilege of appearing at the side of the signore and the powerful in the magnificence of their garb and adornments. To those who are especially skillful and enterprising, the signore will concede the honor of taking part, directly or indirectly, in the administration of power. Their words and acts can determine the rise or fall of individual courtiers. Their favor brings one closer to the signore; their disfavor pushes one into the furthest shadows. In a world of gazes and appearances, beauty and the skills of seduction are formidable weapons.

The new Italian court is no exception to this rule. Courtesans, virtually nonexistent prior to the establishment of the new signore's power, or at best relegated to the sidelines, have come into great demand. They call them actresses, starlets, escorts, soubrettes, and a variety of specific Italian terms:

attricette, divette, vallette, veline, and *letterine,* but they are in every other way comparable to the courtesans of bygone days though perhaps, in many cases, less well educated. Some of them have been rewarded with public honors, formally acknowledged, an unquestionable step forward, the product of the emancipation of women. This is not idle gossip, they admit it openly: "Our bodies are our calling cards," confessed one woman who has been elevated to public honors. But shouldn't the overriding consideration be their moral and intellectual qualities, their devotion to the common good? A perfectly legitimate and appropriate question in a well-ordered republic; completely out of place in a court. Other women have only one duty: to appear, for the most part saying nothing, at the politician's side. Their bodies enliven the grey drabness of the powerful, and they emphasize their theatrical talent. Their presence underscores the weightiness of important events. When a leader concludes a conference or an important session, the courtesans array themselves around him, circling his brows with a symbolic crown of laurel, or they line up beneath the podium, so as to exalt his potency.

In moments of leisurely amusement, alongside the courtesans, there is the minstrel who entertains with his songs. His name is Mariano Apicella. If his music and his compositions meet with approval, all the doors swing wide open, all eyes swivel to him. The applause is merely the first reward; it is followed by other benefits, first and foremost that of remaining at court. Could the new court lack a minstrel? His entrance into court is triumphal: it is none other than the signore in person who presents the new minstrel to the courtiers foregathered for dinner in one of his palazzi. He is capable of playing and singing any melody imaginable, accompanying himself on the guitar. He brightens the evenings with his own songs or other songs he has composed together with the signore, and those are of course the most roundly applauded. He not only performs in the private palazzi but also on television or else in the presence of other sovereigns, during state visits. The signore did not hire him; he adopted him. His gesture was one of generosity toward a son of the little people, a young man who was making ends meet by working as a car-parker in Naples. "President Silvio Berlusconi," the artist declares, "opened the doors of celebrity to me." This is one of the purposes of a court.

For the most momentous gatherings, there is an anthem to be sung together, with enthusiasm. Apparently the composer is none other than Berlusconi himself. The lyrics, no more than thirty or so words in all, are in the distinctive language of the new court: act, believe, grow, "history is what we make it," the future lies open, a beating heart, the power of hands joined together, strength, and rebirth. The first verse runs: "Come on, let's stand up / with powerful hands / let's stand up / the future lies open / let's all go into it / and your hands clasped in mine / so much energy / to feel so much greater"; but another variant runs like this: "Come on, let's all go in / with powerful hands / let's stand up / your energies joined together with mine / a future / to feel ourselves more open." Or else like this: "Come on, my future / to feel so much greater /

let's all go in / and your hands open to my / energies / so we can all stand up, united more than ever." Anyway, the words don't really matter much, what matters is singing the song all together in the presence of the signore. Once the old political anthems, so rich in history, were forgotten, the new ditty, Ceccarelli assures us, entered easily into the brains of millions of Italians.[33] And yet it is "soulless," like an advertising jingle. And precisely because it is soulless, it is perfect for a nation of courtiers who identify themselves with their signore.

While there is no official buffoon at the new court, there is no shortage of courtiers who are eager to render themselves ridiculous, in some cases out of a deep-seated vocation, but more often in order to comply with the orders—explicit or implicit—of the signore. The setting of course is one of his magnificent properties, where the court is deployed in all its splendor. One example might be that of Emilio Fede, when he joins in the rejuvenating ritual of a healthy run, led by the signore. In the midst of his athletic endeavors, the devoted seventy-plus-year-old courtier trips and falls headlong, offering a pathetic spectacle to the photographers lurking in ambush. Is it possible that a man his age should be reluctant to spare himself the ordeal of running in the hot sun of August?[34] The signore was there, the very man who dispenses such enormous benefits and reputation to him, the man with whom his own identity is so completely bound up. How could Fede have disappointed him by proving himself incompetent at the ritual of the daily jog, so necessary to staying physically fit, as the signore demands of both himself and his courtiers?

No sacrifice is too great, not even the sacrifice of one's dignity, in order to remain in close proximity to the signore and to comply with his wishes. The journalists report that powerful cabinet ministers willingly agree to recite, aloud, in the evenings together, passages of texts written and selected by the signore. Once they have completed the collective reading, there is the task of going over the songs, likewise composed by the signore with the assistance of the court minstrel. Then there is the obligation to laugh when the signore tells jokes. There are those who laugh too loud and too long in their excessive zeal, and they make themselves ridiculous, but these are pitfalls into which one may easily fall. The signore, perhaps inadvertently, perhaps intentionally, does not hesitate to humiliate his courtiers publicly. News reports tells us that during a conference he ordered the president of the region and the regional director of the party to get up from their chairs and he commanded them to hold a chart on which he presented the major public works he intended to implement. He went on at length, completely indifferent to the two politicians standing there, one of them the elected head of a public administration, humiliated by being used as human pedestals.[35]

Let the reader try to imagine how such statesmen as De Gasperi, Ugo La Malfa, Enrico Berlinguer, or Aldo Moro, to offer just a few names,[36] might have reacted to an order from the prime minister to put on a pair of shorts and run along after him, recite passages written by him, sing his ditties, or hold display boards for his public orations. They would have looked at him with pity and disdain. Whatever defects they may have had, they were not courtiers and they were not mentally dependent. The courtiers of the new court instead are eager and willing to comply, perhaps with a little muttering, the occasional complaint, though of course under their breath, and never in the presence of the signore. It also makes it easier to understand the hidden resentment and the ill-concealed rancor that often appear on their faces, as well as the arrogance and the aggression that they eagerly discharge in the direction of free men and women, those who stand up straight, who have not bowed down to the caprices of a signore. The populace or, as we say nowadays, the "folks" who watch the spectacle of the court in fascination, admire them and want to become like them, in the hopes of winning fame, honor, and riches. Thus the court penetrates deep into the body of the nation, and with it comes servile manners of thought, speech, and action.

3

THE SIGNS OF SERVITUDE

Servants can be recognized by a number of unmistakable signs. The first, as political writers tell us, is fear. Someone who lives under the arbitrary power of another man never feels safe, even if he is not oppressed, because he knows that the man who is dominating him can take his life, or humiliate him, or deprive him of his property. He is downcast, he doesn't look other men in the eye, he is inclined to lie and dissimulate, and most important of all, he is incapable of courage. In contrast, the distinctive mark of political liberty is the sentiment of security and safety, understood as the absence of fear. In the masterful cycle of paintings by Ambrogio Lorenzetti in the Sala dei Nove (Hall of the Nine) in the Palazzo Pubblico, or City Hall, of Siena (1339–41), fear looms over the city that is dominated by a tyrant, while security reigns over a free city. The same concept is found in Machiavelli, as well: the "common utility that is drawn from a free way of life," he explains "is being able to enjoy one's things freely, without any suspicion, not fearing for the honor of wives and that of children, not to be afraid for oneself."[1] It would be Montesquieu who later went on to introduce in the classic work of modern liberalism, *On the Spirit of the Laws*, the concept that while the principle of tyranny is fear, the principle of a republic is tranquility of spirit: "Political liberty in a citizen is that tranquillity of spirit which comes from the opinion each one has of his security, and in order for him to have this liberty the government must be such that one citizen cannot fear another citizen."[2]

Because it is neither tyranny nor a despotic government, Berlusconi's power is not maintained by fear instilled in the subjects. He has shown that he can relegate to the sidelines the people who oppose him openly, and he relies on dissuasive lawsuits for damages from defamation against those who accuse him of great wrongdoing. In general, though, he leaves his opponents freedom to express their opinions and to criticize him. He defends himself with the immense power of his communications media, not with police repression. More than instilling fear, he wants to persuade, as well as buying people with favors. In short, in contrast with Machiavelli's advice, he wants more to be loved than feared, convinced, I imagine, that in this way he will obtain more glittering glory.

Along with fear, another distinctive sign of dependency is servility, that is, the inclination to indulge a powerful man in order to obtain or maintain privileges. Tiberius had just risen to power, Tacitus, the historian of imperial Rome, narrates, and "at Rome people plunged into slavery" (*ruere in servitium*). Consuls, senators, knights, and the most illustrious were the most eager and the most hypocritical, with a careful studied expression lest they express glee at the death of Augustus, or afflicted at the beginning of the new reign, they mingled tears, smiles, lamentation, and adulation. One of them, Messala Valerius, went so far as to propose "that the oath of allegiance to Tiberius should be yearly renewed, and when Tiberius asked him whether it was at his bidding that he had brought forward this motion, he replied that he had proposed it spontaneously, and that in whatever concerned the State he would use only his own discretion, even at the risk of offending." This, Tacitus comments, "was the only style of adulation which yet remained."[3]

That example from classical antiquity however has been outdone in our own time when a Rome city councilman felt called upon to propose dedicating a street or a square to Silvio Berlusconi's mother in appreciation "of an ordinary person who, through her dedication, helped to write a page of our recent national history by contributing to the decision her son made to enter politics. A decision that has been approved over the past sixteen years by millions of citizens. It is in fact fundamental that we should not overlook the memory of those ordinary people who, with their courageous everyday contributions, have brought about a radical transformation in our country."[4]

No one, as far as I know, ever suggested dedicating a square or a street to the mother of Garibaldi, Cavour, Mazzini, or Carlo and Nello Rosselli, or any other great Italian. But as a senator under Tiberius put it, certain ideas spring directly from the imperious command of our moral conscience, certainly not from the desire to flatter a powerful son. Let us now read a few pages written by the Italian minister for culture Sandro Bondi, keeping clearly in mind that the first rule of a good flatterer is to proclaim himself a friend and not a flatterer: "My sentiments are authentic and are stained neither by hypocrisy nor adulation. The fact that I love Ber lusconi does not mean that I lack my own political independence." Furthermore: "A party must support the leader but not take his place. Allow me to offer an example. On the subject of abortion, I took a very strong position, alongside Giuliano Ferrara. But Berlusconi offered freedom of conscience and did not want Forza Italia to follow too emphatic a line in terms of ethical and moral positions. So I took a step back, calibrating my positions differently, so that they would be more in line with Berlusconi's positions." Finally: "I never say no to Berlusconi. But there's always a genuine exchange of ideas between us."

The claim to possess independent judgment however does nothing to undercut the profound inner identification: "He addresses me with the informal *tu*, I address him with the formal *lei*. I can't bring myself to address him as *tu*. But deep in my heart I know that the *lei* is transformed into a *tu*, in a sentiment that transcends this life of ours. It irritates me when there are people who don't know him well at all and immediately address him with the *tu* and call him Silvio. That really annoys me." Alongside that identification, there must necessarily be a certain willingness to accept sacrifice: "At the times of the harshest ideological and political polarization between the left and Berlusconi I had to throw myself bodily between them." Nor, of course, should there ever be any unwillingness to exalt the unrivalled greatness of the signore: "Berlusconi did something miraculous, prodigious. In just a few months' time he founded a party, routed the enthusiastic war machine led by Achille Occhetto [the general secretary of the Italian Communist Party who transformed the party into the Democratic Party of the Left], won the elections, and became premier. Something no one could ever have imagined. He had sensed that a vacuum had come into being in Italian political life in the aftermath of the collapse of the Berlin Wall and especially after the Tangentopoli (Bribesville) scandals. A vacuum that he could fill"; "life and liberty are two fixations that guide Berlusconi's actions. I don't know whether life or liberty matter more to him…. He is absolutely devoid of a faculty for hatred or the ability to harbor negative feelings toward other people. Even toward people who have done him harm…. He has a natural predisposition toward the expansion of life, a bent for irony, imagination, and fantasy"; "He cannot be compared with anyone else because he is an absolutely new and original political leader."[5]

An even more eloquent document on the spirit of servility that enormous power generates is a transcription of the telephone call between Berlusconi and Agostino Saccà, general manager of the RAI broadcasting company. Despite the fact that Berlusconi was not yet prime minister at the time, and was the leader of the opposition to the government of Romano Prodi, Saccà addresses him with the formal "lei."

Berlusconi in contrast uses the informal "tu," clearly indicating their respective positions. After the conventional preliminaries, Saccà offers an egregious model of the technique of magnifying the glory of the powerful:

> S: President! *Buona sera*... how are you... President...
>
> B: We're surviving...
>
> S: Eh... well sure, but surviving spectacularly, I mean to say, you have your challenges, that is, I... you are still the most beloved one in the country...
>
> B: Politically speaking, we're at zero...
>
> S: Sure.
>
> B:... Socially speaking... they've taken me for the pope...
>
> S: In fact, I was saying, you're truly beloved in the country, look, I say this without the slightest flattery...
>
> B: I've become the target... the object of attention I don't deserve...
>
> S: Eh... but it's stupendous, because it's what we needed... there's a vacuum... that... that you are filling, emotionally as well... that is it means... so that people... really... that's how it is... we register this...
>
> B: It's sort of embarrassing...
>
> S: Wonderful, though.[6]

The effort made by journalists on television to celebrate the signore has been particularly determined and effective. The TG1—the evening news broadcast on the lead public network—on 12 April 2009, Easter Sunday, a week after the earthquake that devastated L'Aquila and a number of neighboring towns is a document of the propensity of journalists, even those who do not work for Mediaset (the television network owned by Berlusconi), to present their reports in such a way as to exalt the virtues of the signore. At 10:22 p.m., the television camera shows a close-up of a toothless old woman saying: "I was embarrassed to look at the President... I had to put my hand over my mouth... I said, forgive me, I have no teeth"; voice-over of the journalist Emma D'Aquino: "Anna, age seventy-three, has become an ambassador for San Demetrio, a village destroyed by the earthquake. Her story begins when she met Prime Minister Berlusconi." The journalist's voice continues, "There are so many people who have lost everything in the earthquake, and they ask the politician for all sorts of things. She tells Berlusconi that many other old people just like her lost their dentures in those terrible moments." Now D'Aquino speaks directly to Signora Anna: "What did the president say to you?" Anna: "Eh, to tell the truth, I was overwhelmed, I didn't hear a thing." Evidently disappointed at the vagueness of her reply, the journalist suggests a better answer to the old woman: "Did he tell you that he'd help with your teeth?" "Yes he said the help... order the dentists, I don't really know... I heard something like that, but I didn't pay too much attention, you see... I didn't think he was referring to me." The journalist insists: "But in fact he was referring to you and no one else..." (images of doctors standing in front of an ambulance fill the screen); "From

Rome a group of doctors from the Istituto Eastman made a brand new dental prosthesis for her in just a few hours" (images of doctors placing the new dental prosthesis in Signora Anna's mouth). The journalist now speaks to the physician: "But how can it be that it usually takes so much time to make a dental prosthesis and here you did it in a couple of hours?" Alberto Falconieri of the Istituto Eastman answers: "We implemented a number of strategies that make this possible under extreme conditions." Now we see Signora Anna about to climb into a big black limousine. "Are you ready to meet the President?" Anna answers: "And in this car, what an honor... let's go, let's go."

Even if the journalists hadn't seen to it themselves, Berlusconi would be perfectly capable of celebrating his own glory. In a press conference on Saturday, 8 August 2009, he spoke for forty-seven minutes without a break, drawing a summary of the first fourteen months of his government. He asks the journalists—is he joking?—whether they are happy with the editors-in-chief "that I appointed." He says that no government has accomplished in such a short time the things that his administration has done: Alitalia is working, there is social harmony, anyone who loses their job can rely on the support of the state, after the earthquake in L'Aquila, "within four minutes we were on the job, and now many of the people have left on cruises, there is a great contentment among the populace. We are three days ahead of our planning and scheduling. The citizens will have green meadows, flowers, stately trees, sculptures in every garden, and in their refrigerators, they'll find a cake, a bottle of *spumante,* and a greeting card with our best wishes. On their beds, there will be monogrammed linen." He explains that houses will be built in record time, "in part thanks to a stroke of genius on my part, a result of my own experience as a builder: we'll break up the construction contracts and we'll have three shifts, working round the clock." In foreign policy, Berlusconi says: "I managed to halt Russian tanks just two hours outside of Tbilisi, and if I hadn't the world would have slipped back into the Cold War"; he notes that he settled "the colonial question with Libya." He offers a response to anyone who questions the Italian success in the South Stream agreement between Russia and Turkey, signed two days earlier in Ankara: "I worked hard at the request of Putin and Erdogan. We are particularly interested in this agreement because ENI [Italy's public energy company] will have a major role to play." Success in the Middle East, as well: "We secured a cease-fire between the Israelis and the Palestinians."[7]

As is entirely understandable, the signore finds it deeply offensive that anyone should dare to criticize his actions. To a journalist on the TG3 news broadcast who asked him a question, he replied: "You belong to a news organization that yesterday filed four reports all in opposition and contrast with the activities of the government. I believe that is something we should no longer tolerate, that we can no longer tolerate: that RAI, our public television broadcasting company, should be the only television on earth that, with taxpayers' money, attacks the government. We are the majority, we don't want to do what the other left-wing majority did in the past, when RAI continued to attack the opposition... the mandate that I would like to give our public television, which corresponds to the mandate desired by the Italians who pay for RAI (I have very clear opinion polls in this context) with the money of one and all, is that RAI genuinely provide a public service and that it attack neither government nor opposition.[8]

The court is a temple of falsehood, taken in the narrowest sense as a deliberate attempt to conceal the truth. Courtiers lie in order to accuse other courtiers, and especially to insult the enemies of the signore or to defend him from accusations. They know that the more shameless their lies, the more they will meet with the approval of the signore. Among the countless instances we can cite, the case of Fabrizio Cicchitto is particularly eloquent: in order to absolve the signore from the accusation of having offended the Constitution of the Italian Republic, he likens him to a great jurist and a Father of the Constitution, Piero Calamandrei, who was always, in contrast, the most stalwart and tireless supporter and defender of the Italian Constitution. Berlusconi, given his congenital intolerance of any other power that might limit his own, had declared that "the Italian Constitution states that sovereignty belongs to the people, it is the people who vote, and it is the Italian Parliament that makes the laws, but if those laws don't meet with the approval of the party of left-wing judges, then they turn to the Constitutional Court which has eleven out of fifteen members who belong to the left wing. Out of those, five are left-wing because they are appointed by the president of the Italian Republic and, unfortunately, we have had three consecutive presidents of the Italian Republic, all from the left wing. Therefore," he said, "from a safeguarding body, the Constitutional Court has been transformed into a political body that serves to abrogate laws passed by the Parliament. Therefore, today, in Italy, sovereignty has passed from the hands of Parliament to the party of judges."

"A transitory situation," Berlusconi concluded, "since we are working to change it, if necessary through a reform of the Italian Constitution."[9]

Even someone who has read only the first article knows that the Italian Constitution does not in fact state that "sovereignty belongs to the people," but instead states that "sovereignty belongs to the people *and is exercised by the people in the forms and within the limits of the Constitution*" (my italics). Now, among the limits of the people's sovereignty, which is expressed in the form of laws approved by a majority in Parliament, there is, in fact, the Constitutional Court, whose task it is to judge "controversies on the constitutional legitimacy of laws." Berlusconi's words are in my view an assault of unprecedented gravity on the highest authority safeguarding the Italian Republic and on the Italian Constitution, which he took an oath to respect. But Fabrizio Cicchitto steps in to defend the signore against all attacks: the signore is by no means an enemy of the Constitution, he has merely reaffirmed "the ABC's of representative democracy: the citizens elect the Parliament, the houses of Parliament choose the government and who leads the government. Instead, here we see the spread of an idea that subjects who were elected by no one, that is, magistrates, can undermine this order by objecting to laws passed by Parliament with the approval of legislative council." After repeating the signore's lie—that the magistrates of the Constitutional Court are subverting the democratic order rather than defending it in accordance with the provisions of the Italian Constitution—we come to the reference to Piero Calamandrei. Even the respected Father of the Italian Constitution, in his view, openly warned against the danger of "a republic of judges."

The truth happens to be that the great jurist always defended the role of the Constitutional Court as an institution that has the authority to "declare *erga omnes* the invalidity of laws" and saw the Constitutional Court as a fundamental "practical guarantee whereby the individual was enabled to defend his rights against the assaults of either legislature or government." He deplored the failure to create a Constitutional Court—it was only established as an operative institution at the end of 1955—as one of the most serious, indeed, "mortifying," "constitutional failures" that could be attributed to the governing majority that was elected on 18 April 1948. He described the behavior of the governing parties as an example of unacceptable "majority obstructionism," dictated by the awareness that "the entry into existence and operation of the Constitutional Court would be an inconvenient hindrance to the overwhelming power that came with great numbers." When, at last, on 13 June 1956, the Constitutional Court issued its first finding of unconstitutionality,

Calamandrei commented in the newspaper *La Stampa*: "The citizens will know that the Constitution is not just words on a page, that the Republic was not just a mockery…. Along the path of Italian democracy, age-old barriers still stand. Now the Constitutional Court has eliminated a stone along the path: in place of article 113 [of the code of Public Safety, which prohibited distributing or circulating, in any public place, or place that is open to the public, without the license of the local authorities of public safety, any texts or drawings] … Other stones will fall, the opening will become wider."[10]

Calamandrei, the author of the very fine book titled *Elogio dei giudici scritto da un avvocato* (*In Praise of Judges, Written by a Lawyer*), who tenaciously defended the Constitutional Court against the arrogant abuses of the governing majority, is instead transformed, through the efforts of a courtier, into a supporter of the excessive power of the governing majority against the authority of the Constitutional Court. What should be noted in particular in this behavior is not merely the unmistakable misrepresentation of Calamandrei's beliefs, but in particular the courtier's certainty that his words will not trigger a wave of indignation that will harm both him and the signore, but will instead be greeted at court by thunderous applause. At court, in fact, live individuals so deeply branded in their souls by the condition of dependency that they lovingly embrace lies.

The issue of the limitations on power raises the question of Berlusconi's widely proclaimed liberalism. Anyone who has read even just a few lines of any liberal political writer knows that Berlusconi's style and language offend the fundamental principles of liberalism and free-market capitalism, which in fact consists of a profound and closely reasoned mistrust of enormous or arbitrary powers and in a strenuous and determined defense of the limitations of sovereign power. Norberto Bobbio had understood this clearly, when he wrote: "Even though it defines itself as the party of freedom, and indeed the central pillar of the Polo delle Libertà, Forza Italia in no way refers back to the Italian tradition of liberalism. It has nothing in common with the liberalism of Einaudi, just to refer to one of the most important names."[11]

Einaudi in fact believed that it was entirely contrary to liberty to believe that, when the citizens "in a free and secret vote have declared, with a majority of 50 percent plus one vote, that they want thus and such a man to lead the government," "then it's all over. *Vox populi vox Dei*," and the minority has no alternative but "to bow down and obey." If that were not the way it was, the minority "would command the majority." The entire logic of a "democratic government," Einaudi points out, "lies in this simple, naked, and impeccable reasoning."[12] But in such a form of reasoning, which Berlusconi and his men repeat ad nauseam, we see neither the logic of a liberal government nor that of a republican government, since both one and the other hold that the power that comes from a popular vote must be limited and controlled by other powers that derive their legitimacy from other principles, such as, for instance, wisdom, competence, and a tested experience and rectitude in governing the commonwealth.

The citizens, Einaudi warned, can easily send corrupt or incompetent men to the Parliament and to the government or they can even send both: "Does this happen because among the masses there are many ignorant people, people who have no aptitude for judging political problems; or the lazy, who are ready to use the coercive power of the state to live at the expense of those who work hard; or selfish individuals, unwilling to sacrifice the moment that eludes the reasons of the future; or the promoters, eager promisers to the masses of the imminent advent of heaven on earth?"[13]

Where the people is sovereign, the demagogue is a threat, and therefore brakes must be instituted to defend the people from its own weakness: "Where there are no brakes limiting the unbridled power of the political classes, it is likely that the suffrage of the majority will be won by demagogues determined to win for themselves power, honor, and wealth, to the detriment of both the majority and the minority. Those brakes exist in order to *limit the liberty to pass laws and otherwise operate* of the governing political classes *selected by the majority of voters*. In appearance this violates the democratic principle that gives power to the majority; in reality, by limiting its powers, those brakes protect the majority from the tyranny of those who would otherwise operate in its name, and by so doing, they implicitly protect the minority"[14] (my italics). To eliminate all and any doubt, Einaudi explains that "if the principle of the majority really was decisive, legislative and executive command would belong to the majority of the Parliament elected through universal and secret suffrage of the citizens. Within the logical limits of that principle, there is no room for the second house of the legislature, nor for the prerogatives of the head of state, nor for the declaration of unconstitutionality on the part of any higher court of law."[15] But in a liberal and republican regime the principle of majority is *not* decisive, and whoever fails to understand that is either ignorant or else wishes to dominate through the old trick of seducing the populace by telling it that it is omnipotent and that no one must attempt to limit the people's power.

It is entirely comprehensible that the closest collaborators of a political leader should feel admiration and loyalty toward him. But it remains admiration and loyalty among equals and fellow citizens, experienced with proportion and rarely expressed in public. In a court, where the signore is set high above the courtiers, admiration becomes veneration, and loyalty takes on the colors of devotion. To experience those sentiments deep down is not enough, they must be manifested to the prince and to the other courtiers. The most appropriate form is poetry. Among the many poems, Bondi's "To Silvio" stands out for its poetic quality and sincerity of inspiration: "Life savored / Life preceded / Life chased / Life loved / The life vital / Life rediscovered / The life splendid / Life unveiled / Life made new."[16]

The courtier-poet, in this case the cabinet minister Sandro Bondi, is not merely celebrating the signore as a vital force that emanates splendor and rejuvenates life. He is able to evoke accents of true poetry for the other members of the court as well. While the signore is life, the other courtiers are true friends and comrades in the battle for a shared objective. Once the battles are over, the time will come to examine their souls, in the sense of yearning that accompanies the fact that they were unable to share the years of their youth as well.[17] For other courtiers on the other hand, the celebration accentuates the power and, once again, the light and love that offer safe and reassuring harbor for those who are daring the stormy seas of politics.[18]

While poetry is the homage paid by an individual, a collective tribute expressing the sincere gratitude for the good that the signore has dispensed and continues to dispense takes the form of a song sung by everyone together, to the tune of music, which unites everyone in brotherhood. In the shared song, all the differences of social status and of rank within the court vanish in an act of thanksgiving that springs not from self-interest but from sentiment. The anthem "How Lucky We Are that We Have Silvio" is a celebration of the power of the signore who vanquished and baffles our treacherous enemies: "Writers and comedians / have tried their best / The perverse attempt / Of those who have already lost / President, this one's for you / how lucky we are that we have Silvio." Like any great leader, he knows how to instill courage and faith in the future: "Long live Italy / the Italy that chose / to believe a little bit / in this dream / That's why I say / how lucky we are that we have Silvio."[19] More solemn than a song, and better suited to express the identification that a courtier feels with his signore, is however the anthem. With the elimination of the worn-out old political anthems that celebrated and invoked the fatherland, liberty, and equality, the new song is for the signore, by now elevated to the rank of worldwide redeemer. The anthem that is entitled "La Pace può" ("Peace Can Do It") insists once again on the power of the signore who radiates light on the world stage: "There is a President / who's always present / who'll accompany us / We are here for you / heart and soul / a Nobel peace prize / Silvio is great / We are here for you / in a unanimous chorus / a single voice / Silvio Silvio is great."

Where there is a signore, there is adulation. The golden rule of the true courtier, Baldesar Castiglione tells us, is to sincerely love his signore and please him: "Therefore, in addition to making it evident at all times and to all persons that he is as worthy as we have said, I would have the Courtier devote all his thought and strength of spirit to loving and almost adoring the prince he serves above all else, devoting his every desire and habit and manner to pleasing him." Even though he must speak to the prince taking care to ensure that his words are always welcome to him, Castiglione assures us, that does not necessarily mean that the courtier becomes an adulator. He can please and comply with the wishes of the signore without being an "inept flatterer," and be rather a "modest and reserved" adulator who always employs, especially in public, "the reverence and respect that befit a servant in relation to his master."[20] A true courtier and a true friend of the signore then is not he who offers only things that satisfy his ambition and speaks only to please in order to gain advantage from that, but also he who knows how to admonish and reprove, who, in short, "does not have the air of being a flatterer and does not admit being one."[21]

The problem is that the courtiers and the counselors of a signore cannot speak on behalf of the common good but must, Thomas More wrote, "agree with the most absurd saying of, and play the parasite to, the chief royal favorites whose friendliness they strive to win by flattery."[22] By his condition, the courtier is obliged to act frequently in an obsequious and adulatory manner, obliged to recognize that "the most important art of a courtier" is that of "rendering himself servile" and "docile." As Tacitus tells us, at court the best opportunities for advancement are offered "to those who were most propense to slavery."[23] Meanwhile at Rome people plunged into slavery—consuls, senators, knights. The higher a man's rank, the more eager his hypocrisy, and his looks the more carefully studied, so as neither to betray joy at the decease of one emperor nor sorrow at the rise of another, while he mingled delight and lamentations with his flattery.

If we were to cite all the examples of compleat flatterers, who in their flattery claim to be, not flatterers but friends and sincere admirers of the signore, and claim to be "modest and restrained" in their praises, we would fill a large volume with that list alone. Let us therefore cite just one among many. In a publication entitled *Berlusconi tale e quale,* the editor Vittorio Feltri advises his readers that his book does not belong to the class of writing that "suffers from genuflectionitis, which would be an inflammation of the lower back due to the posture of a mandarin in the presence of the emperor" and that, despite "a certain feeling of cordiality toward the One Anointed by the Lord," every page of his book will be inspired with sincerity and irony, "which are not always welcome to courtiers": "we sympathize, but we have painted no halo over his head." The editor describes the signore, with an admirable sense of restraint, as "a politician unlike any other on earth."[24]

The flatterer, in order to perform his duties properly, must also insult, denigrate, and deride the enemies of the prince. The more brutal, cutting, and ferocious his words, the more greatly the flatterer's reputation is enhanced. Now, we see that, by surprising coincidence, those books and essays that criticize the signore are described as being "dimly intelligent," "incredible claptrap," "masterpieces of cervical dysentery." Another master of that art explains the hostility of Indro Montanelli (1909–2001, a major Italian journalist, a partisan fighter, hostile to Berlusconi, shot in a Red Brigades ambush) as the result of unbridled jealousy: behold, the great Indro never forgave Il Cavaliere for having stripped out of his hands "not *Il Giornale*, but the title of champion of what has been called the silent majority."[25]

The prince is primarily concerned with preserving his position of preeminence and centrality. To that end, he looks on people who possess integrity, greatness of soul, and courage with abiding suspicion. If he wishes to continue to dominate, he must surround himself with men who are morally corrupt and incapable of noble and generous actions. His precise and overriding interest therefore is to encourage vice and reward moral corruption, like Julius Caesar, who did not seek out good men, but men suited to his purposes, and who considered truly trustworthy only those who did not hesitate to perform any wickedness he might happen to order. It is not enough that the prince should be surrounded by morally corrupt and venal men. They must also be sufficiently numerous to defend themselves—with the prince in the center—from the hostility of the good and respectable people who despise the court. From the court, the enormous power of one man spreads the servile spirit throughout the entire body of the nation.

A seventeenth-century English republican named Algernon Sidney wrote that a prince always chooses ministers who are willing to comply with his wishes, and this fact is so well known that only people who are willing to serve and allow themselves to be corrupted hasten to offer their services. It is in their precise and vital interests, as well as being a natural inclination, to diffuse as greatly as is possible their way of living. In order to attain that objective they must instill in all the people who are to one extent or another under their power all the cowardice and venality of which human nature is capable. They must likewise employ their finest energies to ensure that the prince himself is increasingly ambitious and possesses all the worst vices in order that they might exploit more skillfully all his weaknesses, in their awareness that an honest and great-hearted prince would not tolerate their presence for even a day.[26]

Corruption reigns and will always reign where those who have sovereign powers support it and encourage it, and where it easily receives the most sought-after rewards and is least likely to be—or is never—punished. The greater the power that needs that corruption and which can reward and protect it, the more it can strengthen itself and spread. Liberty and corruption are irreconcilable for the obvious reason that a corrupt people cannot protect itself from arbitrary or enormous powers. By contrast, the power of the court system wants people who are not interested in serving a principle or an ideal or a constitution but a man, and it wishes to select from among the many who have chosen servility as a way of life. The most common reward in the court system is money. The closer a courtier is to the center, the more he will enrich himself. The first consequence of this system is that those who stubbornly insist on not making wealth the primary goal of their lives are scorned and mocked. The second consequence, to limit ourselves just to the most obvious ones, is the spread of criminal behavior. The courtier's way of life demands enormous outlays of money in order to underwrite the pomp and circumstance. The courtiers and the courtiers of the courtiers always need more money, and in order to procure that money, they must break the law. Theirs are lives dominated by vainglory, not by the reason that recommends living without pomp. In order to satisfy their all-devouring hunger for appearance and admiration, they are willing to beg for the prince's favor, steal, corrupt, and allow themselves to be corrupted. If, instead of a prince seeking courtiers, there were councils that rewarded only those who excelled in virtue, the entire system of corruption would dissolve due to a lack of vital nourishment.[27]

Modern-day Italy offers tangible evidence that the considerations of republican political writers about the marks of servitude generated by the court system are still as relevant as ever. The ease with which the worst candidates, in terms of rectitude and competence, are elevated to the highest honors by Silvio Berlusconi is before the eyes of one and all. Let us consider the example of two men who are closest to the center and the summit of the court, Cesare Previti and Marcello Dell'Utri. Previti was sentenced on 4 May 2006 to six years in prison for corrupting judges, a sentence that was rendered definitive. That crime is particularly heinous in that it not only damages one of the parties involved in the trial, but undermines the very foundations of legality, which is in turn the ultimate bedrock of republican liberty. Once judges have been corrupted, the powerful can impose their will. It would be reasonable to expect then that in a republican regime such an individual would be faced, not only by the harsh sanctions of the law, but also by the civil and sober, yet austere and firm, moral repulsion of the citizens, foremost among those who have the honor of occupying the highest offices of the state.

But the exact opposite is what happened. There was a moving groundswell of solidarity. Journalists report that when the news of the sentence came down, the outgoing president of the Chamber of Deputies embraced Previti warmly. In the days that followed, when Previti was confined in Rome's Rebibbia prison, his cell "became the destination of an incessant pilgrimage of leading members of both Forza Italia and the Casa delle Libertà. Arriving one after the other were the president emeritus of the Italian Republic Cossiga, the president of the Senate Pera, Senator Guzzanti, the honorable members of Parliament Cicchitto, Bondi, Pecorella, Tajani, Lainati, Craxi (the daughter), Gardini, Cantoni, Giro, Simeone, Marini, Jannarilli, Cicolani, Barelli, and Antoniozzi, the undersecretaries Santelli, Grillo, and Di Virgilio, the regional councilor Sammarco, the chief of Berlusconi's secretariat, Valentino Valentini, and Paolo Cirino Pomicino in the role of tour guide: he knew the way."[28]

After five days in a prison cell, the prisoner Cesare Previti returned home. The corrections (or surveillance) judge then allowed the convicted member of Parliament two hours every day of unmonitored freedom, "to take care of the indispensable requirements of life." Before the convict could be expelled from the Chamber of Deputies, as required by law, a year went by. When the Chamber of Deputies finally found a way to perform its duty, only a very few members of Parliament rejoiced that justice had finally been done. Their voices were drowned out by the loud protests and avowals of solidarity. There were even those who in an excess of servile spirit went so far as to compare the corruptor of judges to Jesus Christ: "Barabbas was acquitted and Jesus Christ condemned, and the sentences were carried out, even though we all know with the benefit of hindsight how unjust both cases actually were."[29]

The entire story of Cesare Previti demonstrates that in a court regime willingness and skill at breaking the law are useful talents for those who wish to be elevated to service close to the signore. In order for this to happen, the companions of the powerful change the meaning of words to absolve the powerful from accusations and to condemn their accusers. This is the reflection of the corruption of judgment that the wisest political writers have so often denounced. Machiavelli, to cite just one of many examples, emphasized that in corrupt cities "harmful men are praised as industrious and good men are blamed as fools."[30] So it should come as no surprise that through the effect of the courtier's mindset the criminal becomes the victim, and the judge becomes a henchman and tyrant. The examples of the deformation of judgment could be infinite in number. Let us limit ourselves here to a description of Clemente Mastella, a minister of the republic, who stated in Parliament that "between love for my family and power, I choose the former."

These words demonstrate first and foremost that the minister neither knew nor understood the Constitution on which he had taken his oath of office. The Constitution, in fact, orders its representatives to place the republic above the family. It is perhaps praiseworthy that a citizen should consider his family to be more important than the republic and resign from the government, but it would have been even more praiseworthy if he had not accepted any public responsibility, given that his (legitimate) beliefs made him entirely unworthy of the honor that was conferred on him. He should have said, if anything, "between my family and the service of the republic," and not made the distinction between his family and power, because being a minister—to a citizen who is thinking clearly and properly—means first and foremost placing oneself at the service of the commonwealth, and only in second place exercising power. The minister's speech was greeted by a long and warm applause, from both the majority and the opposition parties, a clear sign that the perversion of political judgment had permeated all the political forces.

Marcello Dell'Utri was sentenced on a definitive basis by the Turin tribunal to two years and three months imprisonment for issuing false invoices and tax fraud in the management of the Publitalia corporation (for that crime he was held in a state of arrest for eighteen days in May 1995 and he plea-bargained a sentence in the Court of Cassation). The money he obtained through that fraud was used to pay for the renovation of his villa on Lake Como. He was then sentenced to two years in prison, by a lower court, and by an appeals court, in Milan, for Mafia-affiliated extortion, and to nine years, by a lower court, in Palermo, for external complicity in a Mafia-related conspiracy. The verdict issued on 11 December 2004 by the judges of Palermo is an exemplary document for an understanding of the way in which the court system rewards and elevates individuals capable, in the view of the judges, of the worst kind of wicked actions, and therefore easy to detect and control. Let me quote only two passages:

> The investigation conducted in the course of the trial focused on facts, episodes, and events that extended over a span of nearly thirty years, and that is, from the

earliest Seventies to the end of 1998, when the trial had been going on for about a year, and it explored the previous convictions by the two defendants over that considerable span of time, and in particular, it analyzed the evolution of the career of Marcello Dell'Utri from a young student with a degree in law to a modest but ambitious employee of a savings and loan in a small town on the outskirts of Palermo, to an associate of his friend Silvio Berlusconi (whose siren song he was unable to resist, giving up a secure position in a bank and moving away permanently from his hometown of Palermo), to the administrator of a company in a state of controlled bankruptcy of the group headed by Filippo Alberto Rapisarda (with whom he had, by his own admission, a love-hate relationship), to the position of mastermind and creator of Publitalia, the advertising arm and financial marshaling yard of Fininvest, as well as the organizer of the nascent political movement Forza Italia, and on to national member of parliament in 1996, member of the European parliament in 1999 and, finally, to senator of the Italian Republic in 2001.[31]

Along with great ambition and a willingness to serve powerful men, an invaluable quality of a courtier is an eagerness to recruit men who have broken laws. Once again, it is the judges who note this aspect of the human type of the courtier:

Moreover, the panel of judges considers particularly grave the conduct shown by the defendant during the course of the trial, with respect to the attempt to contaminate the evidence against him... as well as the circumstance that he, relying upon his friendship with Mangano, asked him to do favors in relation to his entrepreneurial activity.... Last of all, we must consider as negative evidence his openness toward the Mafia-related organization in the field of politics, in a historical period in which Cosa Nostra had displayed its criminal savagery through the commission of grave massacres, clear indications of a larger subversive plot against the state, and moreover, when his standing as a public figure and the responsibilities involved with the institutional offices he took on ought to have demanded of him even greater perspicacity and moral rigor, requiring that he avoid all and any contamination with the Mafia-related milieu whose activities he knew very well from his previous history bound up with the exercise of his high-level managerial activities.[32]

Let us admit, for the sake of analysis, that the judges overdid it, and that the defendant was simply a man who failed to take adequate care in avoiding all contact with La Cosa Nostra. Even so, the fact remains that such men could receive the highest honors only in a system that had at its center and its summit a man who had only one objective, that of increasing his own power, and who therefore could not tolerate around or beneath him people that he was unable to bend to his own will. If, instead, the people examining their life history had been individuals dedicated to the service of the common good, who were therefore well aware that their presences in the highest offices of the republic would be pernicious, they would have kept them at arm's length as far as possible. In the United States, to clarify the difference between the spirit of the court and the republican spirit, President Obama fired three high officials in his administration due to minor violations in the compilation of their tax returns; in Italy someone who has been found guilty of aggravated bribery of judges becomes a cabinet minister and someone who has been found guilty on a definitive basis of fraud and on a nondefinitive basis for external complicity in a Mafia conspiracy is made a member of the Chamber of Deputies, the European Parliament, and the Italian Senate, where he still serves. The very idea of political responsibility has long since vanished from our public debate and nowadays it's more or less only the magistrates who seem to have any interest in demanding rectitude in the actions of the signore and his courtiers.

I could continue for many pages providing documentation on the integrity and moral qualities of the people who have attained high honors, but it would be pointless. The mere fact that people with the life histories and personal qualities that I've described should have attained the highest offices and won great fame demonstrates that the enormous power of a signore has once again generated the court system, and it matters little that it was in the context of a democracy. One might well object that men with stories in their pasts similar to the ones I've mentioned here have attained the highest public honors even when the enormous power of a single man did not exist in Italy. That is a serious objection and should be taken into consideration. Even in the past, the republic rejected the best and rewarded the worst, but the new court does so with greater determination and greater consistency. Berlusconi allows only men like those described to get close to him and to attain the splendor of the court. The very few people of spotless integrity and intellectual worth who attain public honors do so only because the signore is unable to thwart them, even though it should be said that his opponents behave even worse than him in many cases, promoting to the highest offices people who can boast as their sole credentials and qualifications only their faithful service to one powerful man or another.

The other sign of the consolidation of the court system, alongside the triumph of the worst men, has been the spread of corruption. After the two-year period of Mani Pulite ("Clean Hands" the code name for the investigation program against corruption set by Milan's prosecutors), political corruption became invisible and therefore much harder to fight.[33] Nonetheless, the data available suggest that the system of corruption has become much more refined. The rankings of Transparency International—the prestigious international nongovernmental organization founded in 1993—placed Italy forty-second in 2004; in 2006 it dropped to the forty-fifth rank. In 2005 alone, those reported and arrested for corruption and for malfeasance numbered 580, to which we should add another 253 for extortion and bribery, 703 for embezzlement, and 204 for misappropriation of public money. A 2006 survey, again by Transparency International, reveals that 48 percent of those interviewed believe that the Italian government fails to undertake decisive action against corruption; 11 percent believe that the government encourages it. In 2006, it is worth reminding the reader, the second Berlusconi government ended its time in power.

With the electoral victory of the Casa delle Libertà (the electoral coalition led by Berlusconi) on 13 May 2001, men took seats in the Italian Senate and Chamber of Deputies who had been found guilty and sentenced, variously, on a provisional or definitive basis. Aside from Berlusconi himself, among those elected were Cesare Previti, Marcello Dell'Utri, Umberto Bossi, Giorgio La Malfa, Massimo Maria Berruti, Gaspare Giudice, Giuseppe Firrarello, and Vittorio Sgarbi, along with other new names who had been protagonists of the Tangentopoli investigations and older names with prior convictions. Particularly emblematic is the case of a candidate elected in the Italian region of Puglia (Apulia) on the lists of Forza Italia who never even had a chance to set foot in the Chamber of Deputies because while undergoing treatment in the hospital he was served with a warrant for his incarceration by the Italian Carabinieri. He had been sentenced to a total of three prison terms amounting to six years of incarceration, for extortion, corruption, receiving stolen property, and illegal financing. As is logical, the court system rewards with special attention those who have rendered personal services to the signore. And so the personal defense lawyers for Berlusconi and Previti are given parliamentary seats. In this way, the trusted right-hand men of the signore are at the same time legislators and his defenders. If their skill at defending him from the laws proves inadequate, then they will arrange to defend him by passing new laws. In a Parliament where some ninety individuals sit who have either been found guilty and sentenced, or else charged with criminal offenses, or else are under investigation for criminal offenses, it shouldn't be hard to find the votes to change the laws to make it easier to corrupt, defraud, and steal.[34]

Now laws arrive that protect present courtiers and encourage future courtiers. At the opening of the 2001–6 legislature, the Parliament approved a law that modified the approach to international letters rogatory—crucial tools whereby prosecutors obtain evidence from their international counterparts—making them much more difficult to obtain and far less effective as probative elements in the judicial system. What makes it even worse is that the new regulations apply to trials now underway as well. It is a law that declares invalid and unusable all documents from foreign judicial authorities that are not either "originals" or authenticated with a stamp on every page. If the only evidence against the defendant consists of documents transmitted from outside of the country, then the defendant must be acquitted. In order to understand what all this means in terms of investigations and trials against the corrupt and the corruptors, we need only consider the words of the chief prosecutor of Geneva: "It's impossible to transmit the original of a bank statement:

all that we ever possess is a printout, which is by definition a copy. The original is in the hard drive at the bank, and that's not something we can very easily transmit to Italy."[35]

The history was similar, and the logic too was analogous, in the case of the law approved on 28 September 2001 concerning the falsification of accounts. From a "dangerous" crime it was reclassified to a "harmful" crime; the maximum penalties, already mild, were reduced even further; it became even easier to run out the clock with its statute of limitations (the limits are reduced to seven-and-a-half years for publicly traded companies and to four-and-a-half years for privately held companies). For privately held companies, the falsification of accounts can only be punished if a suit is brought by shareholders; for publicly traded companies prosecution can also be brought officially by a prosecuting magistrate. Last of all, the authors of *Mani sporche* (*Dirty Hands*) inform us, if you exclude from the balance sheet up to 5 percent of the annual operating results or up to 10 percent of the market valuation, or up to 1 percent of the net assets of the company, the law cannot act. Here, neither the capitalist system nor political ideologies have anything to do with it. The Bush administration, after the Enron financial scandal, increased the penalties for falsification of accounts to a maximum of twenty-five years imprisonment. The crucial difference here is the court system and its vital necessity of having an army of courtiers loyal to the will of their signore.

The efficacy of the court system expresses itself not only in the ability to reward corrupt courtiers, but also, in the ill-omened case that one of them might run into actual trouble with the law and face a verdict and sentence, in the ability to restore them to power. The data speak volumes. The Mani Pulite (Clean Hands) investigation produced, between 1992 and 1994, thirteen hundred findings of guilt, part of them outright guilty verdicts, part of them plea bargains on a definitive basis. The percentage of acquittals ranged between 5 and 6 percent. Of the rest of the cases, some 40 percent of the defendants avoided a sentence through procedural norms or special laws, and nearly all of them, no matter the result of their trials, either remained in public life or quickly returned to it. There is even the case of a politician who made a plea bargain for a significant number of months in prison for a variety of corruption charges, only to enter triumphantly into the Italian Senate. Even more significant is the case of Renato Farina. Former deputy editor of *Libero*, expelled from the newspaper guild after he confessed that he had collaborated with the Italian secret intelligence service by publishing false news reports in exchange for cash, he has been a member of the Italian Parliament, sitting since 2008 in the Chamber of Deputies, in Berlusconi's electoral ranks, and he contributes regularly to *Il Giornale*. The return to court is the prize given for services rendered and a guarantee of further benefits for any future services he may perform.

4

~

THE PREREQUISITES OF SERVITUDE

Over the centuries, the Italians have shown a distinctive capacity for inventing new and unprecedented political and social systems. As the Middle Ages were coming to an end, they gave rise to the first republics since those of classical antiquity. Nearly a millennium later, they created first an ideology of Fascism and then a Fascist regime, neither of which had ever been seen before. Likewise, the transformation of a republic into a great court is an experiment that has never been attempted or accomplished before this. Why in Italy of all places?

A first answer comes in the form of the observation that the court system and the mentality that is an expression of that system both have deep roots in Italy. While the human type of the citizen has always struggled to flourish in Italy, the type of the courtier has enjoyed a long and glorious history, sanctioned by the popularity of the literary work, *Il libro del Cortegiano* (*The Book of the Courtier*) by Baldesar Castiglione, who sketched out the traits and features of that model. Although Castiglione idealized things to a certain extent, he certainly made no attempt to disguise the fact that the courtier, however happy and even proud he might be of his work and his status, is still inevitably a man who lives in dependence on another man, and that this other man is an almost absolute arbiter of his happiness and prosperity. Although Italian history has had moments and examples of moral greatness and a sincere love of liberty, for many centuries it has been a history of servitude, variously in thrall to foreign masters, despotic governments, and the spiritual and temporal dominion of a church that employed both the word and alongside it the sword and the gallows; at times the Italians have been oppressed by all three at once. A long familiarity with servitude has shaped Italian mores, which—it is well known—constitute the most tenacious of all social forces. The writers who have examined the mentality of the Italians with particular perspicacity have left us eloquent portraits. Giacomo Leopardi, who was writing at a time when no form of civil liberty existed in Italy, save as a memory or nostalgia for bygone centuries, explains to us that the principal trait of the servile soul is how little respect it has for itself and for others. Even if it may seem strange, servants have no self-respect; they sense that they have little worth and so they willingly accept their condition. The lack of self-respect brings with it indifference: "A profound indifference, deep rooted and effective both toward oneself and toward others, is engendered by those inclinations and this is the greatest blight in terms of customs, character, and morality." Indifference generates "a full and continuous cynicism of soul, thought, character, customs, opinion, word, and action."

Servants sense the paltry nature and the futility of their condition in life, but they lack the wit and the courage to face despair head on. Since they must go on living and resign themselves to their lot in life, they choose as the best option to laugh at everything, first and foremost themselves: "Now the Italians, generally speaking, and with the diversity of proportion that we must assume in the various classes and individuals, since we are talking about an entire nation, have entirely embraced this course of action. The Italians laugh at life: they laugh far more and with greater truth and intimate conviction and disdain and coldness than any other nation. This is quite natural, because life is worth less to them than it is for others, and it is certain that the livelier and more hot-spirited characters, such as those of the Italians, become chillier when they are thwarted by circumstances more powerful than their own forces. So it is with individuals, and so it is with nations. The upper classes of Italy are the most cynical of all their peers in other nations. The Italian lower classes are the most cynical of any lower classes."[1] In their souls, there is no room for imagination or for the illusions that nourish the generous ideals of liberty and drive men to action, even to self-sacrifice. They scorn the great men who possess those ideals, and with consummate ability they mock them.[2]

The true Italian vice is the lack of inner liberty, the liberty that springs from an intimate conviction that a person's self is a good so precious that no price can be set on it, and it can therefore never be sold to other men. This good is what has been called over the centuries a moral conscience, that is to say, that inner voice that tells you that *your* principles, the principles that make you a particular person, are these and not some others. A person who experiences inner liberty acquires a fierce pride that prevents her from becoming the servant of other men. This idea was stated with fine precision by Piero Martinetti, one of the few university professors who refused to submit to the humiliation of the loyalty oath that the Fascist regime imposed in 1931: "Among the essential duties of man, Kant includes the duty of pride, fierce moral pride. He says: 'Be no man's servant!' And this means: Do not subordinate your conscience to the hopes and fears of life here on earth: do not debase your personality by bending it slavishly before other men! Only those who feel in themselves the need for this moral dignity, for this unyielding pride, are men in the true sense of the word: the rest are a flock of sheep, born to serve."[3]

The finest men of the anti-Fascist movement understood this, that they were in the presence of the lowest forms of servitude to which a people without inner liberty could descend. Carlo Rosselli, in a letter to his brother Nello, wrote that Croce had been right when he said that Fascism was an expression of "a murky state of mind, a mix of a lust for pleasure, a spirit of adventure and conquest, a frenzy for power, a restlessness and at the same time a disaffection and an indifference, *all typical of those who live in an uncentered way, those who have lost that center for a person that is an ethical and religious conscience*" (emphasis is Rosselli's). That is why Rosselli indicated as the cause of Fascism the absence of inner liberty: "Now it is sad to have to admit this," he writes in *Liberal Socialism* (1928–29), "but nonetheless it is true: in Italy, the training of the individual, the formation of the individual as the basic moral unit, is still to a large extent unaccomplished. Because of poverty, indifference, and a long-standing resignedness, most Italians still lack a sharp and deep-rooted sense of autonomy and responsibility. The state of subjection that lasted for centuries makes the average Italian vacillate between the habit of servility and anarchic revolt even today. The concept of life as a struggle and a mission, the notion of liberty as a moral duty, and the awareness of one's limitations and those of others are all missing."[4]

Many anti-Fascists laid responsibility for Italian moral weakness on the church. Ernesto Rossi especially lambasted the sharp contrast between the morality of the Gospels, and in particular the Sermon on the Mount, and the behavior of priests. Christ said:

> "But thou, when thou prayest, enter into thy closet, and when thou hast shut thy door, pray to thy Father which is in secret" [Matthew 6:6]. *And the throngs of the faithful go to pray in famous sanctuaries, special places, convinced that their prayers will be heard there better than elsewhere.* "But when ye pray, use not vain repetitions, as the heathen do: for they think that they shall be heard for their much speaking" [Matthew 6:7]. *And the devout repeat dozens and dozens of times the same Hail Mary, counting the beads of their rosaries to*

be sure that they have reached the proper number. "But I say unto you, Swear not at all.... Neither shalt thou swear by thy head, because thou canst not make one hair white or black. But let your communication be, Yea, yea; Nay, nay: for whatsoever is more than these cometh of evil" [Matthew 5.34, 36, 37]. *And all Christians swear, and the priests themselves swear oaths upon the book of the Gospels which contains this prohibition.* "Lay not up for yourselves treasures upon earth.... Ye cannot serve God and mammon" [Matthew 6:19, 24]. *And when the liberal revolutions came to confiscate the goods of the clergy, the clergy possessed in all the countries most of the finest lands and the most reliable revenues; and even today the clergy continues to reconcile with the greatest nonchalance service rendered both to God and to Mammon.* "Ye have heard that it was said by them of old time, Thou shalt not kill.... But I say unto you, That whosoever is angry with his brother without a cause shall be in danger of the judgment" [Matthew 5:21, 22]. "Ye have heard that it hath been said, An eye for an eye, and a tooth for a tooth: But I say unto you, That ye resist not evil: but whosoever shall smite thee on thy right cheek, turn to him the other also" [Matthew 5:38, 39]. "Ye have heard that it hath been said, Thou shalt love thy neighbour, and hate thine enemy. But I say unto you, Love your enemies, bless them that curse you, do good to them that hate you, and pray for them which despitefully use you, and persecute you"

[Matthew 5:43, 44]. *And in the name of none other than the Gospel, in support and defense of these words of brotherhood and peace among men, baptism has been imposed upon entire peoples with destruction and the sword, the heretics were exterminated, countless, truly atrocious wars were waged; and even today the military chaplains say Mass with the Gospel on the altar, surrounded by cannons, and all the priests of the various nations at war pray to the Lord for the victory of their armies.*[5]

This was the same accusation leveled by Salvemini in 1929:

A great many Italians believe firmly in the Madonna. In fact, they pray to Her continually, and equally continually they blaspheme against her with a richness of imagination and vocabulary that has something wonderful about it. They also know, and they also therefore pray to and blaspheme against, an infinite array of saints, male and female. They also believe in purgatory, and so they pray for the unfortunate souls who must wait to be purged before they can be admitted into paradise, but they never blaspheme against them, never curse them, because they are in the afterlife roughly equivalent to what the proletariat is in this world, and towards them they feel a profound elective affinity, foreseeing that, if it all goes well, nine times out of ten they too will be needing recommendations in prayers, and not blaspheming. They care little about Jesus Christ. So true is this that they blaspheme Him fairly rarely. And as for God the Father Almighty Creator of Heaven and Earth, they find him in the credo along with Pontius Pilate; but who ever thinks of Him or of Pontius Pilate? This state of affairs long predates the Gospels; and therefore the Gospels are not responsible. After all, how many people have ever read the Gospels in Italy, even among those who know how to read?[6]

The Italians are morally weak because they do not recognize the authority of conscience. They do not listen to their conscience, and they do not consider it to be an infallible and inflexible authority. Instead, they have become masters in the art of deceiving their conscience or silencing it with indulgences, confessions, and mental restrictions.[7] "This," Salvemini wrote,

is the most atrocious aspect of moral teachings as imparted by the popes and the clergy: that they develop the vile aspects of human nature, accustoming it not to be aware of its own responsibilities, but instead to place the final decisions in the hands of a priesthood that offers, not the advice of a friend, but the absolution or condemnation of a judge. It is only after having lived in Protestant nations that I have fully understood what a moral disaster for our country Catholicism has been: not the abstract Catholicism, which includes 6,666 forms of possible Catholicisms,... but instead that form of 'moral education' that the Catholic clergy

administers to the Italian people and that the popes insist be administered to the Italian people.[8]

The country's age-old moral weakness, further undermined by Fascism, could not be healed by the birth of the Italian Republic. Emancipated servants do not become free citizens, but freedmen: unfortunates who, as Piero Calamandrei effectively described them in 1945, "still bear on their wrists the bruises of the chains worn for twenty years and in their backs the curvature of the spine caused by a habit of bowing; and they are unable to feel the new duties of liberty." More than sixty years later, we must sadly acknowledge that a sizable number of Italians have not yet risen from the status of freedmen to citizens but rather regressed from freedmen to voluntary servants.

Nonetheless, this explains only in part the affirmation of the court system. To understand it better, it is worthy taking in hand the theory of the political class that was formulated at the end of the nineteenth century by Gaetano Mosca. The central point of this theory is the idea that in all societies, no matter what the form of government, a minority always prevails over a majority:

> Among the constant facts and tendencies that are to be found in all political organisms, one is so obvious that it is apparent to the most casual eye. In all societies—from societies that are very meagerly developed and have barely attained the dawnings of civilization, down to the most advanced and powerful societies—two

classes of people appear—a class that rules and a class that is ruled. The first class, always the less numerous, performs all political functions, monopolizes power and enjoys the advantages that power brings, whereas the second, the more numerous class, is directed and controlled by the first, in a manner that is now more or less legal, now more or less arbitrary and violent, and supplies the first, in appearance at least, with material means of subsistence and with the instrumentalities that are essential to the vitality of the political organism.[9]

In response to the argument that it is unclear how the few can always prevail over the many, Mosca sets forth a peremptory consideration: "The power of any minority is irresistible as against each single individual of the majority, who stands alone before the totality of the organized minority. At the same time, the minority is organized for the very reason that it is a minority. A hundred men acting uniformly in concert, with a common understanding, will triumph over a thousand men who are not in accord and can therefore be dealt with one by one. Meanwhile it will be easier for the former to act in concert and have a mutual understanding simply because they are a hundred and not a thousand."[10]

In a system of representative democracy, an organized minority can easily get itself elected and become a political class, if it follows a single leader and possess sufficient money and resources to communicate its ideas to the majority. That is exactly what happened in Italy in the early nineties. A man who possessed great wealth gathered around him a small group of followers selected from the employees of his companies and particularly devoted to him; with great skill, he made use of the television networks and the publications that he owned; he ran for office and the majority of the electorate voted for him, which made it possible for him to gain control of the government. Still, the prophetic note was sounded as well. One evening, toward the end of the year, Berlusconi recounts in his brief autobiographical pamphlet, *Una storia italiana* (*An Italian Story*), which was mailed out to every family in Italy in 2001, how his mother looked him in the eye and said: "If you feel it is your duty to do this, then you must find the courage to do it." From that moment on, according to the pamphlet, Berlusconi's mother was always at his side in this political undertaking, always ready to encourage him.

Money, devoted employees, television networks, and his mother's blessings would still not have been enough for Silvio Berlusconi if his good fortune hadn't also given him an invaluable and unhoped for piece of help: the lack of a political class capable of fighting him wisely and with determination. He won, in other words, because of the betrayal of an elite whose duty it was to prevent him from accumulating so much power. This is not the first time this has happened. In the past a fair number of liberal and democratic regimes have been suffocated by antidemocratic movements, and the principal responsibility has belonged not to the populace but to the political, military, financial, and religious elite. As Nancy

Bermeo clearly demonstrates in her fine book, *Ordinary Citizens in Extraordinary Times: The Citizenry and the Breakdown of Democracy*, even in cases where significant sectors of civil society pushed for the defeat of democracy, it was always the elites who delivered the mortal blow. In five out of thirteen cases of the destruction of liberal and democratic regimes in Europe, between the First and Second World Wars (Italy, Germany, Greece, Romania, Yugoslavia), the dictators did not in fact seize power but were asked to govern without the consent of the majority. In the political elections of 1921, the National Bloc controlled by the Fascists won 19.1 percent of the votes; the Socialists received 24.7 percent, the Popular Party received 20.4 percent, the Liberals, 7.1 percent, the Liberal-Democrats, 10.4 percent. Even if we don't count other minor political forces, the majority went to the anti-Fascist parties. The problem was that Italy had a king, and that king, instead of declaring martial law and ordering the Carabinieri out against the Black Shirts, summoned Mussolini to form a government.[11]

The exact opposite took place in other countries, such as Finland, for instance, where in the early thirties an aggressive nationalist party, the Lapua Movement, arose. When the movement staged an armed march on Helsinki in 1932, the conservative president P. E. Svinhufvud proclaimed a state of emergency, issued an appeal to the population over the radio, gave orders to mobilize the army, whose leaders immediately voiced their support of the nation's institutions, and declared the Lapua Movement to be illegal. Leading members of the commercial and financial elite also spoke up in defense of the liberal institutions. As a result, the Lapua Movement was defeated and Finnish democracy survived.[12] What was lacking in the democracies that collapsed, in contrast, was the capacity on the part of the political elite to use all the political, economic, and military power available to them against the subversive movements. A clear dissociation issued and maintained with absolute firmness, then, is the most effective weapon in defense of democratic and liberal institutions.[13]

The movement of Forza Italia and the governments led by Silvio Berlusconi are very different from Italian Fascism and from the extreme right-wing movements in Europe during the thirties. I cited the examples of the collapse of the Italian liberal regime and the defeat of the neo-Fascist movement in Finland (I might also have mentioned the case of Czechoslovakia in the thirties and Venezuela in the fifties) in an effort to isolate the interpretative concept of the existence or lack of the capacity on the part of the political elite to establish a certain distance—a rejection—of movements and parties that threaten the solidity of liberal and democratic institutions. In my opinion, Silvio Berlusconi succeeded in his campaign to create an enormous power in Italy in part because he found the way left unguarded by a political elite that was unwilling or unable to establish a certain distance from him—reject him—with absolute intransigence. Whether it was that the elite was unwilling or unable to stop Berlusconi doesn't much matter. In politics, as Machiavelli tells us, you must look at the end, that is, the practical outcome of actions. They didn't stop him, and they therefore failed in their duty to preserve and reinforce republican life in Italy.

That there was no rejection has been amply documented. He never could have become the owner of a television broadcasting empire without the active support, with only a very few exceptions, of the entire Italian political class. That story has already been told very well, and it's not worth going back over it here. Let me limit myself to exploring a few facts and a few images that document eloquently the betrayal by the elite. The first is the episode of the decree laws that Prime Minister Bettino Craxi approved in order to allow the local television broadcasters owned by Silvio Berlusconi to continue transmitting on a national scale after the cease and desist order imposed on 16 October 1984 by the magistrates of Turin, Rome, and Pescara. Craxi met with Berlusconi on 17 October and left for London on a state visit. From the capital of the United Kingdom he ordered, despite the advice of Christian Democratic leader Ciriaco De Mita, an earlier than scheduled meeting of the council of ministers for Saturday 20 October, at 10:30 a.m. Not even for the floods in the Polesine, not for the earthquakes in Belice, Friuli, and Irpinia, had a government moved so swiftly. In open defiance of the Italian Constitution, which limits the field of application of decree laws to cases of urgent necessity, the government approved a decree law of an "exceptional and temporary" nature, valid for one year, to allow Berlusconi to resume broadcasting. On 27 November however the Chamber of Deputies pronounced itself in favor of the unconstitutionality of the decree law, which thus went out of effect. This was a slap to Craxi and a momentary stirring of a sense of dignity on the part of the Italian Parliament; nonetheless the deputies were unable to halt the growing strength of Berlusconi's media power. Craxi first went to Berlusconi's rescue with a new decree law on 6 December, then he devised a clever plan to overcome the resistance of Parliament: he softened the opposition of the Italian Communist Party (PCI) by arranging for the president of the RAI broadcasting company Biagio Agnes to promise the PCI that it would have part of the third network (a new national news broadcast and entertainment programming). The maneuver proved successful. The president of the Communist caucus in the Senate announced a relaxation of their past opposition, which amounted to a no vote without subscribing to the proposal for parliamentary obstructionism advanced by leftist senators in the Sinistra Indipendente. If the PCI had chosen to join the parliamentary obstructionism, the decree would have expired. The decision was dictated more by the interests of the party than the interests of the nation. As Giuseppe Fiori correctly commented: "It is not acceptable, in exchange for a few directorships on the third network, to reduce the intensity of attack on a decree law that must be combatted for the protection of a vital interest, a defense of a normal democracy: in fact, this decree law sanctions arrogance, abuse, a challenge to the law, and it legitimizes a private monopoly that, by draining advertising without limit, crushes the local broadcasters who have respected the laws and undermines the print media."[14]

The conclusion was, as could be predicted, the approval of the measures that Berlusconi wanted from the Parliament. The details of this episode are, all the same, important if we wish to understand whose fault it was and how it happened that an enormous power was consolidated in the shadow of the republican institutions. The decisive transition is on 4 February 1985, the last day on which it was possible to convert the decree into a full law or extend it. At this point, perhaps we should listen to the account of the chronicler, Giuseppe Fiori:

> On Monday afternoon, the telecommunications commission continues its session in Palazzo Carpegna. The commission still has to examine the amendments (for each amendment, presentation, debate, and a vote); it must then issue an opinion on the law as a whole with declarations of the votes of the individual groups. When the curtain rises, at 3:05 p.m., a brief cavatina by the chairman, Roberto Spanò. Depressed, clearly out of sorts, he reports that for this series of measures (for which, under normal circumstances—proceedings with a normal degree of seriousness—at least two sessions would have been in order) the time allowed by the presidency of the Senate has regrettably been foreshortened: *in all, twenty minutes.* The commissioners exchange incredulous glances; even representatives of the majority, jealous of an invaluable commodity, their own personal dignity, find unacceptable this mockery of an institution because of the demands of the personal interests of a private citi-

zen who has amassed wealth in illegal conditions. The dismay is followed by protests: in vain. They must hurry to the hall; there work will resume at 3:30 p.m. *Intermission*: from the meeting room in Palazzo Carpegna to the Senate hall in Palazzo Madama is not a short distance. There are memories of the commissioners hurrying along, by leaps and bounds, like tiny figures seen in an old film-viewing moviola when the film is speeded up.

In the hall, "the president of the Senate Francesco Cossiga announces the protocols according to which the afternoon session will be conducted":

> "I herewith report that I have ordered, in compliance with Article 84 of the Regulations, the following harmonizing of the times for speaking..." "Harmonizing" is parliamentary jargon, a euphemistic variant of a more common term that was eliminated because it is slightly jarring: limitation. There is no question that the president has the power to limit the time available to speak; in this circumstance the debate will be over the criteria by which he exercised that power. There are limits and then there are limits: it's a question of proportion. Use or abuse of power? "We are on the verge," reacts [Nicola] Lipari, "of being witnesses to a new form of euthanasia: the euthanasia of a parliamentary form of a state of law."[15]

The Parliament of the Italian Republic bowed to the will of a single man. It deliberated, with a few laudable exceptions, not as an assembly of free men, but as a rabble of servants. It wouldn't have been that bad, if they had acted as private citizens and had freely decided to bow to the will of a single man. But with their vote they laid the foundations of a power that would in time also make all the citizens of Italy servants, the citizens that they had the duty to represent in accordance with the dictates of the Constitution.

A second and particularly eloquent episode took place in the context of the approval of the Mammì, Craxi, Andreotti (and Davide Giacalone the hidden instigator) Law, to give the names of its sponsors. The prime minister was no longer Bettino Craxi, but Giulio Andreotti. In general terms, the law assured Berlusconi three television networks without any regulation governing the collection and placement of advertising. In public opinion and in the halls of Parliament a debate arose over the possibility of inserting commercial breaks at will, even in the middle of movies. During the course of the parliamentary debate, Walter Veltroni (at the time a promising young leader of the PCI, then founder of the Democratic Party) issued this statement, on 18 July 1990:

> One month ago—exactly one month ago, on 18 June— Berlusconi, one of the subjects with interests that are directly affected by this law, announced during the course of a convention of advertising salesmen for Fininvest that there would be (I can exhibit the text) a vote of confidence over the Mammì Law. This was, let me repeat, 18 June. No one had discussed this possibility.

And yet Berlusconi announced it as if he knew that he could dictate the law, as if he knew that he could impose his own will.... It would be paradoxical that our parliament should find itself operating in such a condition of limited sovereignty.... Someone announces a vote of confidence in a setting that to me and to my institutional culture appears improper, namely a convention of Fininvest advertising salesmen. Thus, after the "Berlusconi decree law," we will find ourselves faced with the "Berlusconi vote of confidence." That vote of confidence would appear to be nothing more and nothing less than the implementation of an order imparted.... Minister Mammì, I don't know whether the government will call for the vote of confidence that has been requested and in a certain sense demanded one month ago. I do want to say, however, that it would be an act of arrogance and, if I may, recklessness.[16]

In 1990, Berlusconi already had sufficiently great power to determine a decision by the Italian Parliament. The individuals who sit in the legislative assembly want what Berlusconi wants: they have become, in the true sense of the word, not representatives, but courtiers. The year is 1990, when Berlusconi has plenty of money, television networks, and influential friends, but still lacks a political party all his own and still lacks direct political power. But the particularly significant, and starkly dramatic, moment of the story is a brief exchange of remarks between Senator Massimo Riva, of the Sinistra Indipendente, sponsor and author of the law under discussion; the Republican Oscar Mammì, and the president of the Italian Senate; and Giovanni Spadolini, also a Republican, in fact, a figure of great stature in the context of republican culture:

> Massimo Riva: "In his response, His Honor the Minister has said that he continues to be puzzled why we insist on those proposals to limit commercial interruptions. I believe that I can explain the reason to him quite briefly. We have no problem with disobeying the orders of Cavaliere Berlusconi."
>
> Oscar Mammì: "Nor do I, Senator Riva, and please use a different style of argument!"
>
> Presidente Spadolini: "Senator Riva, allow me to say to you that the expression of thought in a theatrical or cinematic work remains intact whether you see the film without interruption or with some breaks."
>
> Giovanni Berlinguer: "If they put advertisements in the pages of your books, what would you say?"
>
> Spadolini: "By now all magazines have advertisements."
>
> Berlinguer: "I'm talking about the pages of your books."
>
> Spadolini: "Unfortunately one day there will be advertisements even in the pages of my books. In fact, there are a number of ads in many books."[17]

We feel sadness, as well as indignation, when we read the transcript of this exchange that took place in the highest legislative assembly of the Italian Republic. Parliamentarians who proclaimed themselves to be republicans bowed without dignity to the wishes of a man who was powerful because of his wealth. Spadolini had published twenty years earlier *L'autunno del Risorgimento* (*The Autumn of the Risorgimento*); with the words that he uttered on 13 March 1990, he ushered in the autumn of the Italian Republic.

With the approach of the 1994 elections that allowed Berlusconi to become prime minister, his opponents began to become aware of the danger threatening the republican institutions. The late Eugenio Garin wrote for instance that "Berlusconi means the resurgence, not of a conflict between two democratic positions, but of a resumption of the worst aspects of the limitations of Italian political life. The establishment of a right-wing that tends to return power to the Man of Providence (this Italian catch-phrase for Mussolini was a phrase uttered by the pope). Something extremely insidious and old, outside of any clear and unsullied vision of political conflict and peaceful alternation of power."[18] Claudio Magris: "There is a risk of a homogenized Italy, a treacherous and gelatinous authoritarianism."[19] Denis Mack Smith noted that "a man who concentrates in his hands all that editorial power is not my ideal of a democratic liberal.... When you have that many newspapers and magazines, that many television networks, then there is no assurance of a liberty that is equal for one and all. These situations can be, in fact, a grave threat to a liberal democracy."[20] Achille Occhetto, too, just a few days before the elections, emphasized that Berlusconi's enormous power threatened the essence of the liberal state: in case of victory, the owner of Fininvest would have "a power that would allow him to appoint directors of both the private and public television networks, to encourage laws in favor of his own interests.... that's no liberal democracy! Old Montesquieu, with his principle of the separation of powers, would turn over in his grave."[21]

After the defeat, all the same, the belief prevailed that the Berlusconi government would be a right-wing government like many others in a pattern of alternating governments. In the face of the new government, Veltroni emphasized, it would be necessary to lead the opposition the way it had always been with a right-wing government: "responsible, firm, and loyal." As Disraeli once pointed out, Veltroni continued, "No government can be long secure without formidable opposition." What is most striking about these words is not so much the indication of a firm, loyal, and responsible opposition, as much as the belief that the new government would be a normal right-wing government. Massimo Luigi Salvadori notes that the victory of Forza Italia is the first example in Europe of the electoral affirmation of a newly formed party just a few months old, and adds that Berlusconi succeeded in uniting a complex bloc of political forces "under the banner of free-market liberalism."[22]

Norberto Bobbio clearly glimpsed the political significance of Berlusconi's entry onto the Italian political stage, in particular in an article he wrote immediately after the victory of the Ulivo (Olive Tree) coalition led by Romano Prodi on 21 April 1996, when it was reasonable to suppose that Berlusconi and Forza Italia might quickly melt away. Bobbio insisted first of all on the personal, charismatic, theatrical, and courtly nature of Berlusconi's power: "But the absolute and astonishing novelty of Forza Italia lies in the fact that it is—how to put this?—the first personal mass party. Those who voted for Forza Italia did not choose a platform or a program, they chose a person, that gentleman, always elegantly dressed, who is well acquainted with the art of attracting attention to himself with his eloquence, his nonchalant and captivating way of moving and speaking to his audience, even telling a joke now and then, with the skill of an experienced showman; always smiling, self-confident, a skillful simplifier of economic concepts, which he lowers to the point that anyone can understand them; wonderfully talented at painting himself as the victim of plots, conspiracies, betrayals, a naïve target of vicious enemies and treacherous allies. You must have seen him once or twice when, heralded by his anthem, he enters a large room packed with people. When he comes in they all leap to their feet and shout for a few minutes, indeed, they invoke him: 'Silvio, Silvio!'"[23]

Berlusconi's power, in Bobbio's view, has a menacing authoritarian dimension, skillfully concealed by good-natured and reassuring language and manners: "One of the well known and well documented aspects of the 'authoritarian personality' is the absolute confidence in himself, in his own ability to solve the most difficult problems not only for himself but for others as well. His favorite motto is: 'Let me take care of it, I'm working for you.'" Above all he understood that a power of that kind transforms the citizens of a republic into a people of courtiers: "Do you remember the photograph of the cluster of white-clad joggers in track suits who were out on their healthful morning run? Silvio led the pack, his faithful collaborators were running behind him, panting but happily fulfilling their obligation to serve. I recall the witticism of an anonymous observer who saw the vignette and commented: "I had an idea / I'll express it in jest / servants were once garbed in livery / now in track suits they're dressed [*Mi è venuta un'idea / lo dirò con una battuta: / vestivano i servi un dì la livrea / oggi la tuta*]."[24] In comparison with the servants of a bygone day, we might add, the servants of today are millions, almost an entire people.

The perception of danger announced by respected thinkers nonetheless did not translate into the belief that Berlusconi's power might deal a fatal blow to republican political liberty. If there had been such an understanding, the opposition might very well have been more intransigent. Instead, aside from a few declarations that were more for show than serious statements of intent, the prevailing line has been and remains that of a moderate opposition willing to talk and negotiate, especially concerning the reform of the institutions. The first signal of a determination to avoid a head-on clash with the government was the behavior of the opposition representatives on the committee for elections of the Chamber of Deputies, which had been summoned to deliberate concerning Berlusconi's ineligibility for election in compliance with the 1957 law that states that it is illegal for anyone to accept government office who is also the owner of public concessions of significant economic importance. Clearly, the intention of the legislature had been to prevent any unmistakable conflicts of interest. The committee for elections, with a center-right majority, voted against the proposed order of incompatibility with the argument that the true owner of the concessions of the corporations was not Berlusconi but Fedele Confalonieri. More surprising perhaps than the outcome of the vote was the fact that the DS (Democratici di Sinistra) deputies also voted against the application of the 1957 law. Similar behavior appears in 1996, when the committee, this time with a center-left majority, unanimously rejected calls to declare Berlusconi ineligible for membership in Parliament.[25]

Massimo D'Alema, in a discussion with Paolo Sylos Labini, declared that the DS deputies voted in 1994 in favor of ineligibility: "In July 1994 the committee for elections of the Chamber of Deputies rejected by a majority the appeal against the election of Silvio Berlusconi as a member of Parliament. The deputies of my party (a party of which I had only been secretary for a few days) of course voted against that motion, like all the other progressive parliamentarians. Two deputies of the Popular Party, then under the leadership of the Honorable Buttiglione, voted with the majority." To this objection, Sylos Labini replied by citing official documents, page three of the proceedings of the committee for elections of the Chamber of Deputies for Wednesday, 20 July

1994, and pages ten through twelve for Tuesday, 17 October 1996. The parliamentary minutes are indisputable: when they had a chance to apply the law against conflict of interests, Berlusconi's adversaries decided not to do so. They may very well have had their good reasons, but the fact remains: they preferred an attitude of yielding compliance instead of an intransigent policy. Thanks to their actions, Berlusconi was able to further reinforce his power.

All the same, the most eloquent example of the opposition's willingness to seek a modus vivendi with Berlusconi is the story of the parliamentary Commissione Bicamerale (two-chamber commission) for the reform of the Italian state, which began its work on 5 February 1997 under the chairmanship of Massimo D'Alema only to be dissolved in May 1998 without having attained any of its objectives. The chief cause of its failure was Berlusconi's behavior. First he inserted into the agenda of issues to be treated the problem of Italian justice and then, unsatisfied with what he had obtained, he withdrew his support for the Commissione Bicamerale, thus decreeing its demise. In this connection, Sylos Labini commented: "It has been said: D'Alema chose the path of appeasement with Berlusconi because he had the idea of the Commissione Bicamerale, which required good relations with him. He could not, on the one hand, declare open war with Il Cavaliere, undercutting one of his key interests and on the other hand expect to obtain his cooperation. If that is the case, then the error was precisely the idea of undertaking the Commissione Bicamerale with an individual like

Berlusconi."[26] To this argument, D'Alema replied that the Commissione Bicamerale

> was a high point of the reform push. It obliged the right wing to engage in a negotiation that undercut its 'subversive' character as a force for an institutional rupture and brought out articulations and divisions. Above all, it delineated a roadmap for reforms—certainly not without its weaknesses and inconsistencies—which might however have represented a foundation for a major reform to be undertaken in parliament which might have marked a safe landing for the lengthy Italian transition.... It was Berlusconi who broke off negotiations and shipwrecked the plan for the Commissione Bicamerale. This is indubitable evidence that there were no obscure concessions in the plans for reform in terms of principles and values, as has been said over recent years. And it was from this break that his rebound to victory began.[27]

Years later, looking back, I think that we must recognize that Berlusconi's impatience with the controlling institutions that limit executive power only grew more pronounced, as are demonstrated by the words that he uttered in Bonn against the Constitutional Court. And yet, after he openly took that position, there were renewed offers of cooperation and agreement on the part of the most respected opposition leaders. In any civil country the prime minister's words would have produced so indignant and powerful a reaction that he would have been forced to submit his resignation; in Italy his opponents instead announced that they were willing to work with him on a reform of the Italian Constitution. In terms of political realism such behavior is demented; from the point of view of political idealism, it is despicable.

It remains entirely to be seen that there is any urgent need to undertake a reform of the Italian Constitution. It's not enough to accuse anyone who opposes the reform of the Constitution of being a conservative, for the obvious reason that there is no reason to think that conservatives are always wrong just because they tend to approach major changes with great caution, or to think that reformers are always right because they believe that it is reasonable and safe to proceed briskly and at speed. Even if we accept the premise that it's a good idea to reform the Constitution, the fact that this reform must be carried out with Berlusconi ought to be sufficient reason for any political realist to do nothing. But the most important consideration, for the problem that interests us here, is that the episode of the Commissione Bicamerale reinforced Berlusconi. D'Alema himself admits: "And it was from this break that his rebound to victory began." Concerning the DS and D'Alema, then, we must assign blame to them for having helped Berlusconi just when he was particularly vulnerable and for having thus opened the path to him for his triumphal return to government in 2001. Niccolò Machiavelli, who knew something about political realism, warned that enemies must either be caressed or extinguished. Berlusconi's opponents did neither one thing nor the other, with the unsurprising result that they reinforced him and weakened themselves. But did they really consider him an enemy?

The advocates of the politics of understanding maintain that while the "demonizers," that is to say, the advocates of intransigence, actually reinforce Berlusconi, moderation weakens him. In this case too, the facts speak for themselves: after fifteen years of the politics of understanding and agreement, Berlusconi's power has become increasingly great and today (in May 2010) he is capable of proceeding toward his ultimate objective, the devastation of Italy's republican constitution. Aside from the facts, a simple reasoning, once again of straightforward political realism, demonstrates that the policy of intransigence is more effective than the policy of moderation.

The quest for agreement, in fact, alienates the militants—either because it pushes them toward extreme forces or else because it encourages them to withdraw their political commitment—who would otherwise be willing to work on behalf of a genuine political and moral alternative to the power of Berlusconi. This loss is not outweighed by any conquest of electoral support in the sectors of public opinion that voice only lukewarm support for the power of the new court. Enthusiastic and numerous militants on the other hand could win votes both on the left and from the center. One of the many lessons that we can take from Obama's victory—aside from the fundamental lesson that a leader's moral qualities are a real force, every bit as much as money and broadcasting—is that political intransigence leads not only to dignity, but also to militants, and militants bring votes, and votes win elections. Too bad that no one in Italy has understood this yet and put it into practice.

Probably the decision to opt for a policy of dialogue and agreements with Silvio Berlusconi developed more out of a dependency or a sense of moral submission than any political calculations. From the words and the actions of many of the opposition, we detect not a sentiment of moral repulsion with respect to the signore, but instead a poorly concealed empathy and admiration and perhaps even envy for his enormous power. This is shown for instance by phrases that Massimo D'Alema has uttered: "Berlusconi is the best candidate that the right can offer" (1 July 1995); "I trust Berlusconi: I really think that he's sincere when he says that he wants reforms" (23 January 1996); "Berlusconi isn't Beelzebub. He's a nice guy" (12 March 1996); "Berlusconi has brought an important new development into Italian political life" (22 April 1996); "I'm worried by the idea of Berlusconi's government falling, which could lead to the disintegration of the Polo delle Libertà (Pole of Freedoms) and bring an end to the process of building a true alternative democracy" (31 May 1996); "With Berlusconi, we must rewrite the rules of the democratic state" (3 June 1996); "In human terms, I really like Berlusconi" (25 July 1996).[28]

Still more revealing are the opinions of other leaders on the politician who was Berlusconi's mentor and guide, Bettino Craxi. As few people now remember, Craxi was found guilty and sentenced on a definitive basis to five years and six months imprisonment for the ENI-SAI bribes (corruption) and to four years and six months for the bribes involving the Milanese Metropolitana (illegal financing); he was found guilty and sentenced on appeal to three years for Enimont (illegal financing), five years and six months for the ENEL payoffs (corruption), and to five years and nine months for the Conto Protezione (case name for the fraudulent bankruptcy of the Banco Ambrosiano); he was saved by the expiration of the statute of limitations on appeal after being sentenced in a lower court to four years for receiving bribes from Berlusconi through All Iberian; he was a defendant in the lower-court trial for the bribes involving the Milan-Serravalle highway (corruption) and for those involving foreign aid to the Third World, as well as for tax fraud concerning his income from a variety of bribes. To all this we should add the fact that the former secretary of the Italian Socialist Party (PSI) practiced with unprecedented cynicism the most reckless kind of power politics and fought like no one else to give Berlusconi an opportunity to build his media empire. In the end, as if all this were not enough, he fled Italy and died at Hammamet, Tunisia, a fugitive from the law, not an exile.

You might expect from anyone who has even a modicum of love of country an unwavering condemnation of such a personage. Instead, respected leaders on the left have openly rehabilitated him. In the aftermath of the congress in which he had indicated Craxi as one of the guardian spirits of the

DS, the party secretary Piero Fassino told Furio Colombo (a journalist and parliamentarian of the left):

> I've said what I think of Craxi many times. Craxi was an important leader of the Italian left, a leader who harkened back to a sensibility that has always been present in Italian history: Socialist autonomy is a tradition that dates back to Nenni in the years after Livorno. He was a politician who had certain intuitions, and in particular he understood long before many others, and before we did, that Italian society was changing much faster than politics was capable of perceiving. That politics needed to lead the way in the modernization that Italian society demanded. The way in which that intuition was interpreted by Craxi and by the PSI has been the subject of controversy and conflict within the party. To say that Craxi was an important leader of the Italian left is not the same as subscribing to everything that Craxi did. You can't rewrite history, we all know about the tragic aftermath of Craxi's and the PSI's history. But that aftermath cannot force us to erase him from the history of the Italian left, which would be a mistake, nor can it oblige us to identify him solely with the events of Tangentopoli (Bribesville). Craxi is a more complex personality than that, and he should be considered for what he was and what he did. There will be opportunities to debate this, and I believe it would be useful to leave that debate to historians rather than to politi-

cians. It encouraged me that the Congress applauded me when I said: "We are the heirs to a great history that extends from Turati to Nenni and to Craxi": that means that our people clearly understand this statement. I believe that I have done something that is politically honest.[29]

Walter Veltroni echoed his words four years later: Craxi "interpreted better than any other politician the ways in which Italian society was changing." His foreign policy, moreover, "was great. There was the episode of Sigonella but also the decision to keep Italy in the western sphere, without undercutting the autonomy and dignity of the country." Craxi, Veltroni explains, was faced with two much larger parties, one of which was always in the government—the Christian Democracy, or DC—and the other always in the opposition—the Italian Communist Party, or PCI—in a system that suited both of them just fine: the greatest possible stability and the greatest possible public debt: "Craxi decided that it was time to change the rules of the game, confront the Italian left with the problem of a new leadership." The PCI, in the meanwhile, was still struggling under the burden of its old stain, 1956, the invasion of Hungary: "I reread the transcripts of the party meetings, they make your flesh crawl." In the portrait that Veltroni offers, Craxi designed a party that was different from the models of the twentieth century, the PCI and DC, "a fluid, modern party, capable of accepting even things that are not homogeneous to it, but which are

united around certain ideas." The only slight criticism has to
do, not with the monstrous system of corruption conceived
and implemented, but the 1991 referendum on the election
law, when Craxi, instead of urging the Italians to go to the
beach, "should have used that opportunity to encourage bi-
polarism. And the reformation could have taken place only
with a reformist leadership and not with a post-Communist
leadership."[30]

Let me point out, by the way, that urging Italian citizens
not to vote meant exhorting them to neglect a civic duty that
is explicitly indicated by the Italian republican constitution,
which Craxi, as prime minister, necessarily swore to respect.
In the view of the former secretary of the Partito Democra-
tico (Democratic Party), the error was merely one of political
tactics. But there are other questions to be answered, as far
as the reasoning that interests us here: How can a politician
who admires Craxi scorn Berlusconi? And how can a politician who does not scorn Berlusconi pursue a policy of intransigent opposition meant to construct, not another court
with other courtiers, but a true republic? The fact that the
opposition should not feel toward their signore a profound
distance and moral alienation is a sign of the power of the
court system and the worrisome lack, among the political
elite, of a republican culture. Even the most fervent adversaries lack that culture, with the consequence that they do not
oppose the signore for the right reasons, and they easily slip
into the errors of benign tolerance followed by absolution.
Perhaps the most tragic aspect of the Italian reality is the fact

that many enemies of the court aren't friends of the republic. They haven't the foggiest idea of what the liberty of citizens is and as a result they can neither plan nor pursue a political alternative to the liberty of servants.

One truly extraordinary example of the lack of republican spirit in the ranks of the opposition to Berlusconi is an article that Piero Sansonetti, editor in chief of *Liberazione*, the publication of Rifondazione Comunista (Communist Refoundation Party), wrote following the conviction of Previti. Already, the lede is a minor masterpiece in the art of transforming the hostility of a reader with far-left convictions into sympathy by presenting the illustrious convict not as an enemy of the working class but now as a victim of the state: "Cesare Previti is in prison and the matter strikes us as unsettling. A powerful man in a jail cell, a rare event. Are we happy about it? The man for whom in the past five years laws and clauses of every kind of judicial code have been modified, in an attempt to secure his salvation, the wealthy and powerful lawyer, the former cabinet minister, the untouchable member of Parliament, is now locked up in a small cell, with iron bars, a metal door, a cot, and perhaps a gas hotplate that he probably doesn't know how to use." Having painted this word picture, the journalist begins to express doubts about the verdict and the sentence: "He should have been found guilty, I believe, if the evidence was there. I also believe that prison is an excessive abuse, a useless and unjust violence." With a rapid logical leap in his line of argument, worthy of the most classic servile culture that views the law only and always as an instrument of oppression and sees the judges as motivated only by a determination to persecute, he comes to his proposal for a law *ad personam*, a tailor-made law, to be achieved naturally with an agreement between the majority and the minority: "Today, I suggest taking certain steps to allow Previti to leave prison. And I see only one step that is truly serious and coherent and that could also lead—in this climate of such extreme polarization between the right and the left—to a bipartisan operation in Parliament. Let me put it in the form of a one-liner (though not really…): 'a law *ad personam*.' A very special kind of law *ad personam*: amnesty." If anyone should oppose that approach, they would naturally be an extreme reactionary, or even, with a brilliant neologism, a "prigionista"—a prisonist, or an incarcerationist. Needless to point out that admiration for Berlusconi, moral submissiveness, and the absence of a republican culture all work together, reinforcing one another, with the ultimate result that the Italian political elite is unable or unwilling to defeat Berlusconi's power.

5

THE PATH TO FREEDOM

The Italians, at least the better individuals among that people, succeeded in being reborn from servitude to liberty when they developed a healthy scorn for the life of a courtier. It is during the Risorgimento that we find the most impassioned invectives against the court. Even as moderate a political thinker as Vincenzo Gioberti wrote that in the court,

you see "spite in the hearts, falsehood in the faces, sweetness in the words, venom in the desires: contempt for simplicity and a celebration of cunning, an undermining of innocence and shrinking before evil, favor elevated to the stars and merit ground down," as a Jesuit said.... Thus the name of *courtier* is nowadays taken to signify in men a quality that is less than entirely honorable, and in women a shameful position. The courts not only pervert ideas, render effeminate and corrupt the mores, encourage ignorance, false and frivolous learning, idleness, pleasure, pride, and greed on the part of the prince, as well as segregating him from the life

of the citizens, but they often hinder and lead astray
the business of the public, creating in opposition to an
open and juridical government a concealed and illegal
government, altering the distributive justice of ranks
and splendors, unseating good ministers, elevating the
worthless over the worthy, swindlers over the honest,
the wicked over the virtuous, preparing national revolutions with palace coups, and scheming in short to lay
the foundations of an incessant, tireless, effective conspiracy against the better nature of the prince and the
happiness of the fatherland. But to reform and abolish
all courts (although it is not impossible) is far easier to
wish than to execute.[1]

A few years later, Giuseppe Verdi, adding to his words the
immense power of music, had Rigoletto swear the following
curse: "My hate upon you, sneering courtiers!" (*Cortigiani
vil razza dannata!*). Benedetto Croce—and the coincidence
truly is one of those that make us stop and think—reminded
his compatriots, as the long night of Fascism was drawing to
an end, that the rebirth began with contempt for the court.
The "new Italians" who had fought and suffered for national
redemption, detested the Italy of the courtiers, the Italy in
which "the body of political precepts did not go beyond the
recommendation of cunning, not even crowned, as in Machiavelli, by the poetic vision of a man of cunning and violence, who might expel foreigners from Italy and unite the
country into a powerful state. The citizen had been succeeded

by the courtier, the desire to command and govern had been replaced by the desire to serve to one's own private profit, the capital virtue towards that end being prudence with the other allied shrewdnesses and simulations."[2]

Although predictions are always chancy things in the field of politics, it appears unlikely that the enormous power that has been established in Italy can be replaced by a power that is other than that of the court. There is no political leader on the horizon who truly wishes to, or would be capable of, freeing Italy from the courts. I think it is more realistic to imagine a dissolution of the enormous power through the initiatives of courtiers who wish to free themselves of dependency and move toward the center, albeit in the context of a necessarily smaller court, since none of them can ever hope to concentrate in their hands a power comparable to that of the signore who has been overthrown or who has left the political stage.

If this is the future, it is reasonable to hope that we'll see less servility, less flattery, less corruption, and a reawakening of the civil conscience. But it would not be a true emancipation, and we would by no means have warded off for good the danger of the return of an enormous power. If we truly wish to defeat the court, we need to make courageous choices inspired by a profound devotion to the ideal of republican liberty. The only alternative to the liberty of servants is the liberty of citizens, and only a political leader who understands what this liberty consists of and loves it with his whole being will be able to construct in Italy the political and social ethos that is likely to prevent the rebirth of a court system.

I can imagine the objection: wouldn't institutional reforms and new electoral laws be more useful? I respond to that objection that if there is a man with powers comparable to those of the signore who now dominates the center, there are no institutions or electoral laws that can hinder him. A power that can rely on a media empire, unlimited financial resources, and a vast network of supporters united in its own political party can impose its will in any system, whether it is like the current system in Italy, or a presidential system, or a semipresidential system, with majority-based or proportional electoral procedures, or any conceivable combination of the two. An enormous power is always capable of winning popular consensus, and in a democracy whoever has popular consensus will govern.

The situation would be different if it were somehow possible to pass a law—even better if it were a constitutional amendment—that could prevent anyone who is immensely wealthy or who owned a media empire from holding political office. Republics had such laws in the past, and even nowadays there are republics that impose serious obstacles to very wealthy men trying to enter politics. One example is that of Michael Bloomberg, the current mayor of New York City. Bloomberg is an enormously wealthy man, with a publishing operation, a radio network, and a cable television station. He has relied on his own personal resources to spend much more money on his election campaign than any candidate before him. Still, the New York City Conflicts of Interest Board, which can only issue nonbinding opinions but is greatly respected, demanded that he immediately sell all stock that was in any way linked to the city government. He was also prevented from donating computer terminals to a city administration that needed them. As Paul Ginsborg has rightly pointed out, the example of Michael Bloomberg is especially significant because it takes place in America, where big money has always possessed great power in politics and the Supreme Court, with a historic verdict in 1976, blocked a proposed reform designed to limit campaign spending by candidates.[3]

With the Ethics in Government Act (1978), and with the Ethics Reform Act (1989), as well as the Office of Government Ethics, the United States has equipped itself with effective tools to fight conflicts of interest. American legislation not only established the Office of Government Ethics which, as an agency that is independent from the current government administration, has considerable powers of investigation, oversight, and sanction, but can also depend on a public ethics that will not tolerate the mixture of elected office and ownership of the very media that are crucial to winning such office. Rules and practices concern not only politicians, but their families. The wife of President Lyndon Johnson gave up control of a small local broadcasting company in Texas. In the first term of the administration of President George W. Bush (2000–2004), powerful cabinet members were forced to sell stock that could create conflicts of interest with their public duties.[4] Despite the praiseworthy efforts of a number of members of Parliament, there is no serious law in Italy against conflicts of interest. If there is such a law in the future, it will certainly be a useful thing, but we should not place too much reliance on it. An enormous power that knows how to win popular consensus could either eliminate that law or find ways to prevent its application.

Since the court system has shaped society by spreading the servile mentality almost everywhere, the remedy must necessarily be consistent with the ill, that is to say, rediscovering, or learning, the job of being citizens. As challenging as it might be, it is the only way. The first step is to understand the value and beauty of civic duties. What truly distinguishes a free person from a servant and a courtier, in fact, is his sense of duty. A person who has a sense of duty can never become a servant or a courtier for the simple reason that the honors and benefits that he would receive are always inferior in value compared with losing oneself. Such a person can be oppressed by force, but he will not become a voluntary servant. The only liberty that such a person values, and for which he is willing to fight, is that of the citizen, and therefore he will not accept enormous powers, whoever wields them.

Free citizens are the opposite of courtiers and servants because they are neither indifferent nor cynical, but instead live in their own time with a distinct seriousness of purpose. They do not hide behind laughter at the misery of the human condition and the servant's way of life. They smile at the foibles of humanity, but they admire and pursue great ideals. Because of these traits of their inner life, they are capable of fighting with determination and tenacity against the powerful men who offend civil liberty. One example should stand for all others, that of Giorgio Ambrosoli, who was murdered by a hired killer sent by Michele Sindona on 11 July 1979. In a letter that he wrote to his wife on 25 February 1975, he told her:

> You remember the days of the UMI [Italian Monarchic Union], the unachieved hopes of undertaking politics on behalf of the country and not of the political parties: well, at age forty, suddenly, I have engaged in politics and in the name of the state and not for a political party. With this assignment, I have held enormous discretional power at the highest levels and I have always operated—I am fully aware—only in the interest of the country. In so doing, of course, I have created nothing but enemies because all those who have received what they deserved through my efforts are certainly anything but grateful, because they believe that they got no more than what was due to them: and they're right, though if it hadn't been for me, they would have recovered their assets many months later than they did. Enemies, in any case, don't help, and they will do whatever they can to trip me up on some minor niggling detail, and unfortunately, when you have to sign hundreds of letters a day, you can also inadvertently sign

something sloppy. Whatever happens, in any case, you know what you should do and I am sure that you will do a wonderful job. You will have to raise the children and teach them to respect the values we believed in.... Let them be aware of their duties to themselves, toward the family in the transcendental sense that I have of the term, and toward their country, be that Italy or be that Europe. You will do a wonderful job, I'm sure of it, because you're so good, and the boys are great, one better than the other.... It will be tough life for you, but you're such a good kid that you'll come out on top always, and you'll always do your duty, cost what it may.[5]

These are words that make us understand directly the sense of duty that gave Ambrosoli the strength to battle against Sindona's criminal power.

It is necessary to explain patiently that it is entirely senseless to believe that while rights are liberty, duties are a constraint. To have a right means having the freedom to act or not act in a given manner: the right to express your own opinion consists of the liberty to speak or say nothing, and there is no law that can punish us if we decide to say nothing; the right of free association consists of the liberty to associate or not associate, and no one will punish us if we decide to remain on our own and mind our own business; the right to profess our own religious beliefs consists of the liberty to profess or not to profess, and no one will impose on us the duty to hold this or that faith. I could go on listing examples, but there is no reason to insist on the point, since the one conviction on which everyone is in agreement is that having rights means being free: the greater the number of rights, the broader our freedom.

It is also true, however, that if those who possess rights do not feel the duty to limit them with rules, those rights will vanish into thin air. Guido Calogero explained this point with particular clarity: "What rights would other people ever have, if we did not feel the duty to recognize them, thereby restricting our own liberty with a rule? But the highest rule of all these rules is always our own unconditional moral will to understand other people's points of view, to put ourselves in other people's shoes. It is from this dynamic, evidently, that all other essential 'innate rights' derive and all the supreme principles of the ethical and juridical life... ; and so there is no form of active respect toward any possibility of [their] affirmation in life that is not implicit in this radical duty of ours."[6]

Duty is liberty. It is moral liberty, the most precious form of liberty, because without it the other liberties wither and die. To feel a duty means that you believe it is just or unjust to do or not do a certain thing. It is our own conscience, not other people or the state, that tells us that a certain action is right, and that we must therefore perform it, or that it is unjust, and we must therefore refrain from performing that action. Duty cannot be imposed or ordered: "you must" or "you must feel that you must" are meaningless, nonsense phrases. Nor can duty be encouraged with the promise of a reward or the threat of a sanction: "unless you must I will punish you"; "if you must I will reward you" are, once again, empty phrases. Only we ourselves can impose a duty on ourselves or, to use more classical language, only our conscience can command us to perform a duty. Although the two concepts are related, and are often used as if they were synonymous, duties are one thing and obligations are quite another. We should keep this distinction very clear, if we wish to rediscover the path of the liberty of citizens. While duty is a command from our conscience, obligations are the command of an authority. Stated somewhat differently, we answer to ourselves as far as our duties are concerned, and therefore to the inner voice of conscience; as for our obligations, on the other hand, we must answer to an outside command. Operating in accordance with principles that we have established for ourselves is the highest form of liberty, the liberty of someone who is master of himself and obeys no one outside of himself. We are free, not in spite of duties, but because of duties.

Even in the presence of an oppressive power, those who are morally free remain so, and it is from their sense of duty that they draw the moral strength to resist. To an even greater extent, people who experience moral liberty do not allow themselves to be overwhelmed by the seductions of the court because they are not willing to think, speak, and live the way that the signore commands, but instead wish to have *their own* thoughts, *their own* words, and *their own* lives. People never give enough thought to the fact that two powers that are fundamentally different from one another, totalitarian power and court power, still both consider morally free people as enemies: totalitarian power constrains them to silence by force; court power allows them to talk, but drowns them out with the mouthings of servants. While on the one hand totalitarian systems create, alongside happy or resigned servants, also the figure of the subject who experiences the loss of his liberty with great suffering, in contrast a court creates servants who feel themselves to be free and are happy with their condition, albeit with rancors, resentments, and envies, either because they love being relieved of the responsibilities that come with duties, or else because they enjoy privileges denied to others.[7] Among this second group we find the figure of the servant-tyrant: the servant who does all he is able to deny or assault the rights of those who are slightly weaker than him. Humble with the powerful, he becomes arrogant with the weak. He kisses up and kicks down, as the saying goes. If he can inflict abuse and perpetrate harsh treatment, he does so shamelessly.

Any experience of the conquest or reconquest of liberty demands efforts and sacrifices that are even greater than those involved in the routine maintenance of liberty. Those who dominate, whether we are dealing with a tyrannical or totalitarian power, or a regime that is based on favors and persuasion, are never willing to abandon their position of preeminence without fighting back with all their strength. It is necessary to fight them with efforts that only those who see the struggle for liberty as a duty would be capable of exerting. The recollections of those who have fought justly on behalf of liberty all agree that what drove and sustained them in the battle was a sense of duty and indignation, more than any interest or rights. Interest, if anything, would have encouraged them to stay safe at home and take the greatest possible profit from their condition as subjects or servants, or clients. Those who believe that it is self-interest or material need that drives individuals to fight for liberty seem to forget that in many cases things aren't all that bad under the domination of tyrannical or totalitarian regimes, or of courts, if all that one wants from life is prosperity and honors. With a little cunning, a quality that has never been in short supply in Italy, you can more easily obtain benefits from corrupt regimes than from a good republic.

For that reason, the great leaders of movements for national or social emancipation have always placed duties before rights. When he was invited to give his contribution to the preparation of the Universal Declaration of Human Rights, Gandhi replied, "I learnt from my illiterate but wise mother that all rights to be deserved and preserved came from duty well done. Thus the very right to live accrues to us only when we do the duty of citizenship of the world. From this one fundamental statement, perhaps it is easy enough to define the duties of Man and Woman and correlate every right to some corresponding duty to be first performed. Every other right can be shown to be an usurpation hardly worth fighting for."[8] Only a few years later, Martin Luther King Jr. led the civil rights movement in the United States with an appeal to the duty to fight for the freedom and dignity of every human being. In all his speeches, Dr. King emphasized that the moral principle is more powerful than violence, deception, and prejudice, and that self-interest alone is not enough to sustain a movement that must take on a long and exhausting ordeal.

Italian history also shows that only movements led by men and women with a profound sense of duty have been successful in winning the liberty of citizens. They knew well that the Italian problem was a moral weakness, in the elite and in the populace, which grew out of centuries of foreign domination, tyrannical and corrupt governments, and a bad religious education. As a result, the rebirth had to be moral, even before it was political and military.[9] The Risorgimento took place because we had men and women endowed with great inner strength, morally free, and therefore invincible and capable of arousing great political energies. This kind of Italian has also been described very aptly by Massimo Mila, who was a distinguished musicologist and an important figure in the Italian Resistance movement, in reference to the religious anthem of the Risorgimento, "Va pensiero": "Uncommonly gifted with those antennae that allow artists to foretell the future, Verdi was bringing to the stage a new Italian, the Italian of Masaccio, in the frescoes of *The Tribute Money*, instead of the Italian of Botticelli or Domenico Ghirlandaio; the inconvenient Italian of Dante and Machiavelli, instead of the likeable shirkers and slackers of Boccaccio's *Decameron*; the solid upright type of Italian, adamantine, rare enough, it is true, but who exists, and who comes to the fore when the need arises, in the moments of supreme crisis: Francesco Ferrucci, the Battle of the Piave, the Italian Resistance movement. One of those moments was about to be struck by the clock of historical time, and Verdi seemed to know it."[10]

The best political leaders and intellectuals of Italy's Second Risorgimento (as the Italian anti-Fascist Resistance movement is called) acted out of duty. Let's take the case of Carlo Rosselli, for instance. He was educated by his mother, Amelia Pincherle Rosselli, who had been born in Venice in 1870, and who lived her entire life according to the religion of duty: "*Duty*. The mainspring that drove her [his mother's] generation and drove mine as well, suddenly prompting great things. A spring that nowadays, perhaps because it has been overwound, no longer responds, no longer works. But it was from the sentiment of having done one's duty that the heart was filled with an overflowing sweetness, the source in turn of joy and I would almost say ineffable pleasure."[11] Amelia imparted this same religion to her children, Aldo, who volunteered to fight in the Great War and was killed in combat, and Carlo and Nello, murdered by Mussolini's hired killers in 1937. It was precisely from the religion of duty that Carlo drew the inner strength to resist Fascism with absolute intransigence.

What matters is not whether there are many of you or only a few, but rather being at peace with your conscience, even if it means giving up liberty and the love of your family. Those who live according to the religion of duty feel the responsibility of serving as an example, and examples, as we all know, are more instructive than words.[12] Other men and women of the anti-Fascist milieu took their inspiration from the same religion of duty. Among them was Ernesto Rossi, to cite just one name among many possible examples. His awareness of the call of duty continually drove him to battle and to set an example of intransigence in a country populated by men without spines, even though he knew that his sacrifices would never be crowned by victory.

> Whatever the political situation of the future, we are fated to take a licking as long as we live. It's easy to make that prophecy.... By now I know the Italians and their history far too well to nurture any illusions. Cavour was an Englishman, born by accident into a Balkan nation. You can't change in two or three generations the nature of a people accustomed for centuries to ridding themselves in the confessional of all concerns over how to deal with moral problems, and to hand over all dignity of the life of their society to foreign dominators. That doesn't really matter, though. There are those whose job it is to sign decrees, and those whose job it is to die in the trenches or to rot in prison. This too is a division of labor. And it is possible to prefer the second job over the first, if you believe that by so doing you are affirming values that constitute the very foundation of our lives. Force can triumph over any of us individually, but staying faithful to ourselves means handing down to future generations, with an example that is worth

far more than words, what we consider to be the most luminous part of the thought inherited from previous generations—what makes a man truly a man: liberty.[13]

If the objective is to transform freedmen into free citizens, then no moral transaction with the court is possible. No one I can think of has done a finer job of expressing the significance of intransigence than Ferruccio Parri:

> Against Fascism I have no reason for aversion: save for this one peremptory and irreducible reason, which is that I have a moral aversion: it is, perhaps I should say, a thorough rejection of the Fascist climate. Nor am I alone: my anti-Fascism is not the fermentation of solitary acidity. My ideas are the ideas of a thousand other young people, great-hearted fighters in the past, now enemies of the traffic in honors and the rhetorical bacchanalia that distinguish and color the time of the Fascists. Free of any recent responsibilities, intransigent because they are disinterested, intransigent toward Fascism because they are intransigent with their own consciences, these young people are the true antagonists of the Fascist regime, as those who have the immaculate right to stand up and judge that regime.[14]

Anyone who wishes to work on behalf of emancipation must always remain outside of the court and demonstrate with his words and his behaviors that it is his intention not to found another court but to build or rebuild a free polity.

Emancipation from the liberty of servants requires some texts that can show us the path to follow. Fortunately, there is no shortage of such texts. There are plenty of books that teach us what the liberty of citizens is, and identify the institutions and policies and education that liberty requires. The problem is that there is a systematic process of the destruction of written culture that is already underway and has attained notable success. In Italy two-thirds of the population reads neither books nor newspapers. When asked, "Why don't you read?" 6 percent of those interviewed admit: "Because I don't know how to read." The triumph of television has engendered hordes of illiterates who are incapable of understanding the written word, unable to grasp a concept or develop a line of reasoning. Giovanni Sartori reminds us that almost all of our vocabulary, the vocabulary that free citizens must first and foremost understand and master, consists of abstract words:

> The city is something still "visible"; but nation, state, sovereignty, democracy, representation, bureaucracy, and so on, are not; they are abstract concepts, elaborated by abstract mental processes, and they stand for entities constructed by our minds. Other "non-visible" abstractions include the concepts of justice, legitimacy, liberty, equality, law (and rights). Also, wholesale, we might include such words as unemployment, intelligence, and happiness, likewise abstract. And all of our ability to manage the political, social, and economic reality in which we live, and even more our capacity to

subjugate nature to man's will, is rooted exclusively in a *thinking in terms of concepts* that are—to the naked eye—invisible and nonexistent entities.[15]

Beneath a tiny minority that knows how to read and reason, there has sprung up a mass of neoilliterates. Five percent of the population is incapable of reading an elementary questionnaire with phrases such as "the cat says meow." Then there is another 33 percent of the population that gets stuck at the second questionnaire with slightly more complicated phrases along the lines of "the cat says meow, because it wants to drink milk," and which ask the subject to construct a sentence consisting of twenty words. Tullio De Mauro notes that, given these conditions, a substantial portion of the population is not capable of reading, let alone *La Repubblica* or *Il Corriere della Sera*, but even the newspapers handed out free at train, bus, and subway stations. He therefore asks a logical question: "I understand that people who are not aware of these statistics are unruffled by the situation. But people who know about them necessarily are concerned, and they pose problems that go well beyond the realm of the school. As we were saying, these are statistics that call into question the operation of democratic structures. For many years now, we have been arguing about the substantial reality of democracy: is it enough to say that free elections have been held to be certain that this is a democratic nation? What should we say, though, if this system operates in conditions of widespread illiteracy, of diffuse inability to judge programs and platforms?"[16] I reply that a country with such a high rate of illiteracy can indeed be considered a democracy, but a corrupt democracy. In a country reduced to such conditions, the liberty of citizens is rendered impossible for the simple reason that there are few people with the necessary moral and intellectual standards. More than a century ago, the political and intellectual elite began a daunting project in Italy of elevating the underclass to nation. Many men and women, for a variety of reasons, devoted vast amounts of effort to the task of educating the population to a level of civil dignity. Aside from the spoken word, the fundamental instrument was reading. Public lending libraries were opened, useful, serious, easy-to-read books were printed, young people were educated, and schools were set up for adults.

We can argue all we like about the values and shortcomings of this effort, but the fact remains that the effort was made, that it was serious, and that it was pursued over a long-term period. Nowadays, we can see the opposite taking place, that is, people doing their best to destroy what survives of our civic culture and expand as rapidly as possible the *mare magnum* of the ignorant underclass. For a court system, for that matter, there is no more reliable foundation than an underclass that does not know (or does not wish to know) how to defend itself from the new demagoguery that can make use of images as never before in the past. Whatever the case, the essential condition for resuming the path of the liberty of citizens is to revive the written culture and bring, as we were saying, books to the people.

The first book that people should know and love is the Constitution of the Italian Republic, the product of the most painful, tragic, and elevating experience of emancipation of our history. The articles of the Constitution specify the content of liberty both from the institutional point of view and in ethical terms. In reference to the institutional question, we should point out, once and for all, that Italy is *not* a democracy, but a "democratic republic," as we read in fact in article 1 of the Constitution. The difference is a significant one and it has important repercussions in terms of political behavior.

The word *democracy* nowadays suggests—and the court misses no opportunity to reinforce this conviction—the idea of the people, sovereign and all-powerful, master of law and justice. Republic, on the other hand, means the people, sovereign, but limited by the Constitution: with the power to make laws through elected representatives, but not all-powerful and not master, but the servant of the laws. A correct idea of what Italy is, according to the Constitution, defends against unlimited power, be that of a single man, a few men, or the people. It would be necessary, in other words, to understand that the political ideal that ensures better than any other the true antibodies, antidotes, and cures against the liberty of servants is not a democracy but a republic.

The Italian Constitution not only indicates a sound institutional structure, it also indicates a specific set of duties. Precisely because they knew that a people without a sense of duty can easily become a servant, as happened in fact in

Italy under Fascism, the members of the Constituent Assembly took great care to point out that being citizens not only means possessing certain rights but also certain duties. In fact, as early as article 2 the Constitution states: "The Republic recognises and guarantees the inviolable rights of the person, both as an individual and in the social groups where human personality is expressed. The Republic expects that the fundamental duties of political, economic and social solidarity be fulfilled." These words are crystal clear: the rights of men are inviolable; the Italian Republic recognizes them and guarantees them with the force of law, but in turn citizens must discharge certain duties.

The bond that links rights and duties is reaffirmed as well in article 4, where the right to work corresponds to the duty to work: "The Republic recognises the right of all citizens to work and promotes those conditions which render this right effective. Every citizen has the duty, according to personal potential and individual choice, to perform an activity or a function that contributes to the material or spiritual progress of society." Article 30, on the other hand, places duty before right: "It is the duty and right of parents to support, raise and educate their children, even if born out of wedlock." Contributing to public expenditures, as sanctioned by article 53, is a duty to which an implicit right corresponds, that is, the right to enjoy social, civil, and political rights sanctioned by the preceding articles: "Every person shall contribute to public expenditure in accordance with their capability."

Although many Italians have forgotten the fact, the right to vote, a fundamental bulwark of democratic life, is matched by the duty to go and vote: "The vote is personal and equal, free and secret. The exercise thereof is a civic duty" (article 48, section 2). It is worth noting that in the "Proposed Draft of the Constitution" we read that the act of voting is a "civic and moral duty." This is a stronger and more precise formulation than was passed by the Constituent Assembly. Umberto Merlin, of Rovigo, a Christian Democrat, who reported on these articles, explained in the afternoon session of 21 May 1947 the significance of the words inserted in the "Proposed Draft of the Constitution." Merlin emphasized that the Constitution was not meant to be "an educational treatise" but should "certainly teach certain duties, it must be a code of the rights and duties of citizens. Even better if it becomes, as Mazzini desired, a code of duties before it is a code of rights. Now what harm is there if the Commission has won unanimous approval of this formula?... We have stated in solemn form the duty of voting, the duty of a citizen who enjoys the benefits of this democratic regime, who enjoys freedom, who enjoys personal safety, in short a citizen who has once again become a free human being, in this new climate that democracy has created, should take the trouble to go and vote."

The highest duty that the Italian Constitution indicates is the defense of the country. The members of the Constituent Assembly called it, alone among all the duties, "sacred" (article 52). In this way, they intended to underscore its religious significance: religious not because it was commanded by the God of Revelation, but because the duty of defending the fatherland can also require the sacrifice of one's life, and only a person with a religious conception can sacrifice his or her life. For a person without a religious conception, the word *sacred* has no meaning and a "sacred duty" sounds something like a joke or a rhetorical exaggeration. The members of the Constituent Assembly were in no mood for jokes, however, and they had a profound repulsion about rhetorical exaggeration, especially for the overblown rhetoric about the fatherland that Fascism had scattered in all directions for twenty years. When they chose the word *sacred,* they knew what they were doing. They wanted the Italians to consider the duty of defending their country as a sacred duty because it demands self-sacrifice.

The Italian Constitution points out the duty of loyalty: "All citizens have the duty to be loyal to the Republic and to uphold its Constitution and laws" (article 54). It might seem like a redundant statement, since it is obvious that the citizens must observe Italy's Constitution and its laws. But by stating that they have the duty of being loyal to the Italian Republic and to observe its Constitution and its laws, the framers meant to explain to us that the citizens should not act only out of fear of the laws, but also out of an inner conviction. Loyalty, in fact, is a different sentiment from obedience and submission, inasmuch as it entails an inner persuasion that requires us to act on behalf of a principle, even when doing so is burdensome or onerous.

The duty of loyalty should not be interpreted in any case as an exhortation to docility and meekness. The debate among the Members of the Constituent Assembly on this point is quite instructive. In the "Proposed Draft of the Constitution," the corresponding article (article 50) included a second clause that read: "When the public powers violate the fundamental liberties and the rights guaranteed by the Constitution, resistance to oppression is the citizen's right and duty." This second clause was not approved by the plenary session of the Constitutional Assembly. If the Constitution had included the clause on the right and duty of resistance, it would have taught a fundamental principle of the republican ethos.

The republican ethos is in fact based on two principles: the duty to be loyal to the Italian Republic, the Constitution and its laws; and the duty to resist any arbitrary exercise of power. The first duty is a restraint of license and anarchy; the second duty is an encouragement to resist against arbitrary powers. Together, these duties educate the proper mentality of free citizens; alone, either duty is insufficient. The duty of resistance without the duty of loyalty undermines legality, which is the foundation of republican liberty; the duty of loyalty without the right and duty of resistance dissolves the civic pride that is an equally necessary support of republican liberty. Of the two ills—the excess of civic pride that oversteps the bounds of anarchy, and the absence of that pride, which feeds the servile habit—it strikes me as difficult to deny that in Italy the real problem has always been a shortage, not an excess, of civic pride and boldness.

In place of the clause on the right and the duty of resistance, the Italian Constitution, in article 54, features a recommendation on the duties of public officers: "Those citizens to
whom public functions are entrusted have the duty to fulfill
such functions with discipline and honour, taking an oath
in those cases established by law." At first glance, honor and
discipline might seem like principles befitting authoritarian
and hierarchical societies or institutions, and to have nothing
to do with a democratic republic. They therefore would not
be criteria for the behavior of its public officers. In its tradi-
tional significance, honor is a recognition of the superiority
due to a social rank or wealth. In Italy, the expression "man
of honor" actually describes someone who blindly obeys the
rules and the officers of the Mafia, an organized crime structure. But honor is also tribute paid to the particular superiority and excellence that we owe to honest people, only and
exclusively in recognition of their honesty, in particular the
honesty with which they perform their public duties.[17]

A similar reasoning can be applied to the concept of discipline as well. Michel Foucault wrote that in the modern
world discipline means the constraint of the body and the
mind in order to attain an objective imposed by authoritarian and hierarchic institutions (boarding school, barracks,
factory).[18] In this context, discipline is entirely incompatible
with the principles of a democratic republic and cannot be
prescribed as a rule for public officials. But, as with honor, in
this case too there is an older significance to the concept that
is entirely in keeping with the ethics of public officials of a

democratic republic. I am referring to discipline understood as the ability of an individual to subject himself or herself to rules and concerted effort to attain a given and intended goal.

The activity of public officials has a special excellence and value because it is aimed at the public good. Article 98 is explicit: "Civil servants are exclusively at the service of the Nation." Wheareas serving an individual or a number of particular individuals degrades a person, serving the nation and the common good results in the attainment of a certain dignity. The excellence of the objective and the service demands a stronger sense of discipline and honor than we can reasonably expect from other citizens. The Italian Constitution demands of ordinary citizens loyalty and obedience; it demands honor and discipline only from those who have chosen to serve the common good.

The members of Parliament, in particular, have the duty of representing the nation: "Each Member of Parliament represents the Nation and carries out his duties without a binding mandate" (article 67). This means that anyone with a seat in the Italian Parliament or in any legislative council must deliberate and make decisions guided not by the interests of their party, their friends, or their voters, but only by the common good. A politician who admits that he has voted in a certain way in order to obey party discipline, or to serve his friends, or to satisfy his voters, is admitting that he has violated the duty that the Italian Constitution places on him. The principle that the representatives and public officials are at the service of the nation is the core of republican liberty for this reason:

if they are not at the service of the nation but of wealthy and powerful citizens, or if they are not performing their duties with discipline and honor, then the republic will become the domain of arbitrary power, and the weak will have no choice but to submit to the arrogance of the powerful.

The Constitution of the Italian Republic, however rich it may be in ethical content, cannot alone shape behavior while in fact it is precisely behavior that must be shaped. The court and its courtiers, as I have done my best to point out, are the creators of behavior and custom, and we must work to replace the ways of servile thought and life with those proper to a free way of life. It is possible to shape behavior with education, and in particular with civic education. Shaping free people means educating individuals who will never be under our dominion, nor under the dominion of others; people who wish to be themselves and not servants shaped by the words and gestures of a signore; who accept the burden of thinking with their own heads and walking on their own two legs along the path that they have chosen, well aware that even before and above their own family, above and beyond freedom and their personal dignity, there is the Italian Republic, with its Constitution and its laws.

This must be the guiding principle of the education to the liberty of citizens. Guido Calogero was quite right when he wrote that

in a mother who entirely forgets her own fate in her concern for the fate of her child, a mother who focuses on him every interest that she has in the world, the conscience of men rightly see a great example of moral abnegation. But the conscience of men also feels that a mother who can only see the interests of her own child and is indifferent to the children of other mothers, a mother who is unable to harm a hair on her child's head in order to teach him to understand and respect the rights of others, is far less exemplary in moral terms than is a mother who can bring herself to expose her own sons to death in order to defend the children of other women and men. Thus, that conscience places above the ordinary mother the Spartan mother. And since morality is not an objective but a direction in which we move, that conscience will never give the name of morality to that which is less moral, to something that symbolizes a closer destination when there is something that points to a more distant and elevated objective.[19]

The education and formation of a free person should be the result of a confluence of reason, and certain passions. In the first place, an indispensable factor is empirical reason, which gives us specific elements of knowledge, critically assimilated. To be a citizen means taking part in political deliberations of great importance (war and peace, social justice, the environment). For that reason it is necessary for citizens to have at least a general understanding of the forms of government, the way political systems function, political ideologies and theories, the constitution and the history of their country. But even more important than critical and empirical reasoning is moral reasoning, which teaches us how to think about ethical matters, how to distinguish justice from injustice, how to justify a moral decision, how to see the connections between ends and means, and how to talk with one's fellow citizens to seek the rules of a civil way of life by the light of the golden rule: "Do unto others as you would have them do unto you."

Teaching people how to think about moral problems properly is perhaps the most urgent civil responsibility in Italy. Moral illiteracy has attained alarming proportions, perhaps even worse than literary illiteracy. Obvious fallacies of reasoning—"everybody else does it, why shouldn't I?"; "he broke the law, but he also did some good things"; "he's corrupt, but he's also likeable"; "he has no integrity, but he's so intelligent"; and so on—have become commonplace. In a very perceptive essay, Diego Gambetta and Gloria Origgi have documented the comments developed by academics, journalists, and politicians in defense of a case of plagiarism that involved a well-known economist, Stefano Zamagni, a consultant to the pope. It's worth reading them carefully: (1) there is nothing original, everyone plagiarizes, so why bother? (2) whistle-blowers are always worse than their targets; (3) what is the point of targeting Zamagni? They will never punish him anyway; (4) what is the point of blowing the whistle as *you* will pay the consequences? (5) He is a good *barone*, much better than many others, so why target *him*? (6) Zamagni is a member of the left, and you should not weaken the left during election times; (7) Zamagni shows good intellectual tastes as he plagiarizes very good authors, so he does not deserve to be attacked; (8) given that many are guilty of plagiarism, targeting one in particular shows that the whistle-blower is driven by base motives; (9) in addition, an economist suggested an explanation rather than a justification saying that the real author of the plagiarism was probably a student of Zamagni who wrote the paper for him. This would, funnily enough, imply that Zamagni was innocent of the plagiarism, but still that he signed a paper he did not write, written by someone who also did not write it.[20]

Such a form of reasoning, if we choose to call it that, springs from the unmistakable intent of justifying the violation of rules so that one might be treated with similar benevolence if one were in similar circumstances. With the obvious result that the dishonest are rewarded and surrounded by approval and the honest are punished and surrounded by disapproval and often by thinly concealed scorn. It would be easy to show how many and how great the perverse effects of the mentality of absolving others can be in all walks of life in society, be that in big or small business, and in economic life in general. Here all that matters is to point out that this mentality fits in perfectly in a courtly context, where an honest person is a threat to the signore and to the other courtiers. Let it be said once and for all: people who fail to think clearly in the manner I have just described can only live as servants.

It is also useful to teach the value of instrumental reason, which instructs us on how best to adapt the means to an end and how to seek out that which is advantageous, calculating the foreseeable costs and benefits of actions. But an individual who relies purely on this type of reason is unlikely to become a good citizen. It is in fact a kind of reasoning that tells us, for example, that it would be more advantageous for everyone if everyone were to pay taxes according to their income. Instrumental reason, however, also informs us that it would be even more advantageous not to pay your own share of the taxes and let others shoulder their own burdens and your own. We must therefore teach people to place instrumental reason under the guidance of moral reason. But why should an individual do so? Why should anyone set limits for themselves? I believe that the only motivation for an individual, or perhaps I should say for a number of individuals, to place moral reason above instrumental reason comes, not from reason, but from passions, or let me be more specific, from certain passions.

The passions guide our political and moral deliberations and move us to action. It is difficult to persuade the citizens to approve laws in favor of groups or classes that they hate or toward whom they feel envy. Moreover, it is by no means true that the passions always cloud or confuse reason. There are passions that allow us to be farsighted and to make important distinctions. If individuals are to deliberate and act as citizens, they must therefore feel certain passions. The most necessary one is the love of a free way of life and the repulsion for the way of life of a servant. There are many components to a love of liberty: loyalty to the teachings of our fathers and our teachers, the religious belief that man was not born to serve other men but only God, a particular sensibility for harmony and beauty.[21] All of these components, in different ways, contribute to a culture of liberty.

Close to the love of a free way of life we should put love of country, in its highest meaning. We must educate people to feel that they are both Italian citizens, European citizens, and citizens of the world. But it is precisely those people who have the correct concept of country who can most easily become citizens of Europe and of the world. Let us consider the extraordinary prophecy that Benedetto Croce formulated in the closing pages of his *History of Europe in the Nineteenth Century*: "Meanwhile, in all parts of Europe we are watching the growth of a new consciousness, of a new nationality (because, as we have already remarked, nations are not natural data, but historical states of consciousness and historical formations). And just as, seventy years ago, a Neapolitan of the old kingdom or a Piedmontese of the subalpine kingdom became an Italian without becoming false to his earlier quality but raising it and resolving it into this new quality, so the French and the Germans and the Italians and all the others will raise themselves into this new quality and their thoughts will be directed toward Europe and their hearts will beat for her as they once did for their smaller countries, not forgotten now but loved all the better."[22] For that matter, there is a profound theoretical reason that makes it necessary to place the concept of country at the center of one's civic education, and that is that the love of one's fatherland is a form of *caritas*, of compassionate love toward people and things whose beauty, worth, and fragility we can perceive. It is precisely this constellation of passions, sentiments, and reasons that encourages us to engage in care and service, two essential aspects of the life of a citizen.

Alongside the love of liberty, I would place the passion of indignation, understood as that profound sense of repulsion for injustice that is found in the greatest of souls and which is unknown to servile and ignoble souls. To be willing to be dragged through the mud or to overlook it if one's friends are dragged through the mud, wrote Aristotle in the *Nicomachean Ethics* (IV, 1125b. 30–1126b. 10), is the attitude of a slave. Different from compassion, which is pain in the presence of the undeserved misfortune of others, indignation is, in the narrowest sense, a good anger in the presence of injustice, or better yet, the anger of the good: anger directed toward people toward whom it is right to feel anger. Indignation, in other words, is a healthy anger guided by reason and as such it can, indeed, it must also exist in the soul of a meek person. Bobbio called it "the weapon without which there is no struggle that can be carried on with determination, without which, if victorious, we become weak and, when defeated, we give up."[23] It is the virtue of the forerunners, of those who are ahead of their time, those who show that it is possible to fight against and encourage others to follow their example, even when prudence, with persuasive arguments, suggests standing still, remaining silent, accepting the situation, and bowing to greater forces. Those who act out of indignation "exclude self-interest and calculation," and become capable of the "fanaticism" of initiators who possess the enthusiasm of sincerity and who know how to translate thought into action, as Piero Gobetti wrote in 1922.[31]

Intransigence against acquiescence; defense of the Constitution against all attempts (we won't have to wait much longer, and they will win) to distort it into a tool of domination; moral and civil education against politics reduced to nothing more than appearance and the manipulation of power; the love of liberty and scorn for the lures and attractions of the liberty of servants and resignation. These are all concepts that seem old-fashioned, I am well aware, and that will be met with understanding only by a few and by shrugs and sarcasm from most people. That I can accept. Let me only point out that true rebirths—from servitude to liberty—have always taken place through the rediscovery of ancient principles. That is what happened in Italy's first Risorgimento and again in its Second Risorgimento.

Paolo Sylos Labini concluded his last book, *Ahi serva Italia: Un appello ai miei concittadini* (Servile Italy: An Appeal to My Fellow Citizens), with an exhortation to the political leadership of the left to abandon their acquiescence to Berlusconi and to rediscover the ideals of their youth. It has been five years now, and no one has taken that advice or shown any intention of being willing to follow it. Instead of a greater degree of intransigence, what seems to predominate is a more distinct willingness to be agreeable. Wisdom recommends against repeating appeals. If there is to be an exhortation, let me address it to the great-hearted, those with staunch souls, and let me exhort them to work on behalf of the liberty of citizens to make a simple moral choice, even if that is without hope of reward or victory.

men like Washington, Lincoln, Gladstone, Bismarck, or
reason, I suggest, is the simple one that public opinion
een able to accept the capitalist's claim to be the trustee
interest. It has always seen him for what he is, a special-
-making. It has never really believed that he has a sense
bility outside the narrow limits of his class. He has never
e law as a body of principles above the narrow interests
he has been concerned; he has always been willing, by fair
ul, to secure its interpretation for his special purposes. No
s own way, he has been thoroughly devoted and conscien-
is no reason to doubt the sincerity of his identification of
well-being with the public good. When, as in America, he
judges, state governors, even the presidency itself, he has
the belief that to make them the pliable instruments of his
was the best thing for the American people. He defended
the only way he understood because he genuinely believed
ne right to rule.

ski, *Democracy in Crisis*, London, Allen & Unwin, 1933, pp.

and elsewhere," wrote Norberto Bobbio in 2001, "strictly ide-
ver has diminished a great deal as a result of the crisis in ideol-
all so aware of. But the presence of a candidate who possesses
nse financial resources risks altering the nature of democratic
ney are still democratic, but Forza Italia has such an advantage
resources that it is difficult to consider them democratic elec-
ed on freely given consensus." Norberto Bobbio and Maurizio
Idea of the Republic, trans. Allan Cameron, Cambridge, UK,
s, 2003, p. 79.
rt Elias, *The Court Society*, trans. Edmund Jephcott, London,
well, 1983, p. 90.
sar Castiglione, *The Book of the Courtier (The Singleton Transla-
, New York, W. W. Norton, 2002, p. 24.
te from Carlo Ossola, *Dal "Cortegiano" all'"uomo di mondo,"* Tu-
di, 1995, pp. 102 and 107.
te from Salvatore S. Nigro, *Il segretario*, in *L'uomo barocco*, edited
 Villari, Rome-Bari, Laterza, 2005, p. 96.

Notes

Notes to Foreword

1. Giovanni Sartori, *Il sultanato*, Rome-Bari, Laterza, 2009, p. 127.

2. I am keeping the Italian word originally used to designate the citizen who succeeded in establishing his control over a city in early modern Italian republics.

Notes to Preface

1. Donatella Campus, *Antipolitics in Power: Populist Language as a Tool for Government*, trans. Chris Hanretty, Cresskill, NJ, Hampton Press, 2010; Michael E. Shin, *Berlusconi's Italy: Mapping Contemporary Italian Politics*, Philadelphia, Temple University Press, 2008; Martin Bull and Martin Rhodes (eds.), *Italy: A Contested Polity*, London, Routledge, 2008; Alexander Stille, *The Sack of Rome: How a Beautiful European Country with a Fabled History and a Storied Culture Was Taken over by a Man Named Silvio Berlusconi*, New York, Penguin Press, 2006; Geoff Andrews, *Not a Normal Country: Italy after Berlusconi*, London, Pluto Press, 2005; David Lane, *Berlusconi's Shadow: Crime, Justice and the Pursuit of Power*, London, Allen Lane, 2004; Paul Ginsborg, *Silvio Berlusconi: Television, Power, and Patrimony*, London, Verso, 2004; Jean Blondel and Paolo Segatti (eds.), *Italian Politics: The Second Berlusconi Government*, New York, Berghahn Books, 2003; Stephen Gundle and Simon Parker (eds.), *The New Italian Republic: From the Fall of the Berlin Wall to Berlusconi*, New York, Routledge, 1996.

2. James Walston, "The Bordello State," *Foreign Policy*, 14 September 2010. To my knowledge "whoreocracy" comes from a comment by Nick de Souza in Alexander Stille's article, "The Corrupt Reign of Emperor Silvio,"

New York Review of Books, 8 April 2010. Among the many magazine and newspaper articles, see the famous dossier "Why Berlusconi Is Unfit to Lead Italy," *The Economist*, 30 July 2003.

3. I owe this consideration to the judge Franco Roberti whom I wish to thank.

4. Giovanni Sartori, *Il sultanato*, Rome-Bari, Laterza, 2009.

5. Norberto Bobbio and Maurizio Viroli, *Dialogo intorno alla Repubblica*, Rome-Bari, Laterza, 2001, p. 98; English trans., *The Idea of the Republic*, Cambridge, UK, Polity Press, 2003.

6. See Michelangelo Bovero, *Contro il governo dei peggiori: Una grammatica della democrazia*, Rome-Bari, Laterza, 2000, esp. pp. 127–39.

Notes to Chapter 1

1. Benjamin Constant, *The Liberty of Ancients Compared with that of the Moderns*, in *Political Writings*, ed. Biancamaria Fontana, Cambridge, Cambridge University Press, 1988, p. 311.

2. Isaiah Berlin, "Two Concepts of Liberty," in *Four Essays on Liberty*, Oxford, Oxford University Press, 1969, p. 122.

3. Fernando Savater, *The Questions of Life: An Invitation to Philosophy*, trans. Carolina Ospina Arrowsmith, Cambridge, UK, Polity Press, 2002, p. 95.

4. Thomas Hobbes, *Leviathan*, ed. Richard Tuck, New York, Cambridge University Press, 1996, chapter 21.

5. Berlin, "Two Concepts of Liberty," pp. 129–30.

6. T. Maccius Plautus, *Mostellaria*, or *The Haunted House*, ed. Henry Thomas Riley, accessed at http://www.perseus.tufts.edu/hopper/text?doc=Pl.+Mos.+1.

7. Carlo Goldoni, *The Servant of Two Masters*, trans. Edward J. Dent, Cambridge, Cambridge University Press, 1952, p. 13.

8. Ibid., p. 60.

9. Ibid., p. 86.

10. Niccolò Machiavelli, *Discourses on Livy,* trans. Harvey C. Mansfield and Nathan Tarcov, Chicago, University of Chicago Press, 1996, book I, chapter 58, pp. 115–119.

11. Marcus Tullius Cicero, *De republica*, II.23; I'm quoting from the *Opere filosofiche e politiche*, ed. Leonardo Ferrero and Nevio Zorzetti, Turin, UTET, 1974, vol. 1.

12. The Latin expressio slave are, respectively, "p Chaim Wirszubski, *Libert public and the Early Princ* 1950, pp. 1–15; see also Qu bridge, Cambridge Univer *A Theory of Freedom and (* 1998.

13. Machiavelli, *Discourse

14. Ibid., book II, chap. 2,

15. John Locke, *Second Tr Two Treatises of Government* Ruth Grant, and Ian Shapiro 124, accessed at http://jim.co

16. Jean-Jacques Rousseau *Complètes*, ed. B. Gagnebin an 3, p. 842.

17. Hobbes, *Leviathan*, chap

18. *Ricordi storici di Filippo (tinuazione di Alamanno e Neri* 103.

19. Ibid., C–CV. See in this (pater patriae or padrino?" in Ar *Politica e fiscalità*, Rome, Edizior

20. Machiavelli, *Discourses on*

21. Hobbes, *Leviathan*, chap. 2

Notes t

1. It really is worth rereading w ness tycoons who become politicia

It is, for instance, significant tha tary democracy no great statesm ness man. Like Bonar Law in Eng often held high, even the highest any who has attained the kind of

that came to
Cavour. The
has never b
of the publi
ist in mone
of responsi
regarded th
with which
means or f
doubt, in h
tious; there
his private
has bough
done so in
purposes
himself in
in his divi

Harold L
56–57.

2. "In Ital
ological pov
ogies we ar
such imme
elections. T
in terms of
tions found
Viroli, *The
Polity Pres

3. Norb
Basil Black

4. Balde
tion), I, 17

5. I quo
rin, Einau

6. I quo
by Rosari

7. *Il Malpiglio: A Dialogue on the Court*, Torquato Tasso, trans. Dain A. Trafton, Amherst, MA, Dartmouth College, in conjunction with *English Literary Renaissance*, 1973, pp. 25–27.

8. Ossola, *Dal "Cortegiano,"* pp. 132 and 142.

9. Elias Canetti, *Crowds and Power*, trans. Carol Stewart, New York, Viking Press, 1962, p. 400.

10. Castiglione, *The Book of the Courtier*, p. 223.

11. "The court of a sovereign, a prince, or a seigneur who had jurisdiction over relatively vast territories," wrote Walter Barberis,

> had for the past several centuries represented a point of arrival for many group or individual strategies. It was the stage upon which the powerful performed and showed themselves; therefore, in a variety of forms, it was the crossroads for all ostentation and display, where lineage, luxury, or culture were stylishly exhibited or arrogantly brandished. It was the site of political exchange at its highest level. It was the seat of will and judgment, that is, the power to decide the most serious matters, or else to ignore them, in a counterpoint of institutional maneuvering with the forms of private license. Reality and imagination demanded a mirror-image correspondence between the gravity of the burdens of government and the levity of amusement and distraction. The nobility of rank and the ignobility of sentiments seemed almost necessarily to exist side by side, as well as alongside the extreme forms of a multiplicity of human types standardized only by the coexistence in that exclusive location. Inferno and paradise, in their imagined earthly translation and in their further literary transfigurations, coexisted at court.

Walter Barberis, preface to Castiglione, *Il libro del Cortegiano*, ed. Barberis, Turin, Einaudi, 1998, pp. xviii–xix.

12. Niccolò Machiavelli, *Discourses on Livy*, trans. Harvey C. Mansfield and Nathan Tarcov, Chicago, University of Chicago Press, 1996, book III, chap. 28, pp. 276–77. And even better in the *Florentine Histories*, VII. 1:

> It is true that some divisions are harmful to republics and some are helpful. Those are harmful that are accompanied by sects and partisans; those are helpful that are maintained without sects and partisans. Thus, since a founder of a republic cannot provide that there be no enmities in it, he has to provide at least that there not be sects. And

therefore it is to be known that citizens in cities acquire reputation in two modes: either by public ways or by private modes. One acquires it publicly by winning a battle, acquiring a town, carrying out a mission with care and prudence, advising the republic wisely and prosperously. One acquires it in private modes by benefiting this or that other citizen, defending him from the magistrates, helping him with money, getting him unmerited honors, and ingratiating oneself with the plebs with games and public gifts. From this latter mode of proceeding, sects and partisans arise, and the reputation thus earned offends as much as reputation helps when it is not mixed with sects, because that reputation is founded on a common good, not on a private good. And although even among citizens so made one cannot provide by any mode that there will not be very great hatreds, nonetheless, having no partisans who follow them for their own utility, they cannot harm the republic; on the contrary, they must help it, because to pass their tests it is necessary for them to attempt to exalt the republic and to watch each other particularly so that civil bounds are not transgressed.

Florentine Histories, trans. Harvey C. Mansfield and Laura F. Banfield, Princeton, Princeton University Press, 1988, pp. 276–77.

13. Etienne de La Boétie, *Discours sur la servitude volontaire* (1548), in English, *Anti-Dictator*, trans. Harry Kruz, New York, Columbia University Press, 1942, accessed at http://www.constitution.org/la_boetie/serv_vol .htm. See also the excellent work of Nicola Panichi, *Plutarchus redivivus? La Boétie e i suoi interpreti*, Rome, Edizioni di Storia e Letteratura, 2008.

14. Ibid.

15. Ibid.

16. Tommaso Costo and Michele Benvenga, *Il segretario di lettere*, ed. Salvatore Nigro, Palermo, Sellerio editore, 1991, pp. 99–102.

17. Carlo Goldoni, *The Servant of Two Masters*, trans. Edward J. Dent, Cambridge, Cambridge University Press, 1952, p. 13.

18. Goldoni, "La famiglia dell'antiquario," *Commedie di Goldoni,* ed. Guido Davico Bonino, Garzanti, Milan, 1981, II, 16.

19. Canetti, *Crowds and Power*, p. 400.

20. La Boétie, *Anti-Dictator*.

21. Ossola, *Dal "Cortegiano,"* p. 137.

22. Maurizio Belpietro, *Panorama*, 27 March 2009.

23. Clifford Geertz, "Centers, Kings, and Charisma: Reflections on the Symbolics of Power," in *Culture and its Creators: Essays in Honor of Edward Shils*, Chicago, University of Chicago Press, 1977, pp. 151–71, accessed at http://hypergeertz.jku.at/GeertzTexts/Centers_Kings_Charisma.htm. See also by the same author, *Negara: The Theatre State in Nineteenth-Century Bali*, Princeton University Press, Princeton, 1980, and in particular p. 13, where Geertz writes: "Court ceremonialism was the driving force of court politics; and mass ritual was not a device to shore up the state, but rather the state, even in its final gasp, was a device for the enactment of mass ritual. Power served pomp, not pomp power."

24. Peter Burke, "Il cortigiano," in *L'uomo del Rinascimento*, ed. Eugenio Garin, Rome-Bari, Laterza, 1988, p. 154.

25. Geertz, *Centers, Kings, and Charisma*, pp. 152–53.

26. Filippo Ceccarelli, *Il teatrone della politica*, Milan, Longanesi, 2003, p. 9. See also, concerning the spectacular dimension of politics, Guy Debord, *La société du spectacle*, Paris, Buchet-Chastel, 1967.

27. Ceccarelli, *Il teatrone della politica*, p. 116.

28. Ibid., pp.117–18.

29. Ibid., pp. 113–14.

30. Ibid., pp. 35–36.

31. Ibid., p. 128.

32. Castiglione, *The Book of the Courtier*, p. 150.

33. Ceccarelli, *Il teatrone della politica*, pp. 88–89.

34. Ibid., pp. 113–14.

35. Ibid., pp. 213–15.

36. Alcide De Gasperi (1881–1954, founder of the Christian Democratic Party), Ugo La Malfa (1903–79, an important leader in the Italian Republican Party), Enrico Berlinguer (1922–84, a prominent leader of the Italian Communist Party), or Aldo Moro (1916–78, a prominent Christian Democrat, architect of the entry of the Communists into a coalition government, kidnapped and murdered by the Red Brigades).

Notes to Chapter Three

1. Niccolò Machiavelli, *Discourses on Livy*, trans. Harvey C. Mansfield and Nathan Tarcov, Chicago, University of Chicago Press, 1996, book I, chap. 16, page 45.

2. Charles Louis de Montesquieu, *Spirit of the Laws*, trans. Anne Cohler, Basia Miller, and Harold Samuel Stone, Cambridge, Cambridge University Press, 1989, XI. 6, p. 157.

3. Tacitus, *Annals*, I. 7–8, accessed at http://classics.mit.edu/Tacitus/annals.1.i.html, trans. Alfred John Church and William Jackson Brodribb.

4. Marco Siclari quoted by Maddalena De Bernardi, http://www.tuttogratis.it/attualita/rosa_berlusconi_qualcuno_vuole_dedicarle_una_strada/.

5. Claudio Sabelli Fioretti interviews Sandro Bondi, *Io, Berlusconi, le donne, la poesia*, Rome, Aliberti Editore, 2008, passim.

6. *L'Espresso*, December, 20, 2007, accessed at http://espresso.repubblica.it/dettaglio/Pronto-Silvio-sono-Saccà/1917587.

7. Quotes accessed November 2009 at http://www.youtube.com/watch?v=IUU7dYA3UVM.

8. *Il Corriere della Sera*, 9 August 2009.

9. Quoted accessed November 2009 at http://www.youtube.com/watch?v=1qqRtNQbwWE.

10. Piero Calamandrei, *Questa nostra Costituzione*, introduction by Alessandro Galante Garrone, Milan, Bompiani, 1995, passim.

11. Norberto Bobbio and Maurizio Viroli, *The Idea of the Republic*, trans. Allan Cameron, Cambridge, UK, Polity Press, 2003, p. 69.

12. Luigi Einaudi, *Il buongoverno: Saggi di economia e politica (1897–1954)*, ed. Ernesto Rossi, introduction by Massimo Luigi Salvadori, preface by Eugenio Scalfari, Rome-Bari, Laterza, 2004, pp. 85–86.

13. Ibid., p. 86.

14. Ibid., pp. 87–88.

15. Ibid., pp. 88–89.

16. Sandro Bondi and Claudio Sabelli Fioretti, *Io, Berlusconi, le donne, la poesia*, Rome, Aliberti Editore, 2008, p. 68.

17. *To Fabrizio Cicchitto*: "Let us live together / this unrepeatable experience / with authentic political passion / with a chaste soul / and with the surprise / of friendship. / We will miss one another / when the new time comes / and we will finally be reflected / one in the other. / And we will also miss / what we were unable to experience together / at our desks in school / in our unquiet adolescence / and in the age in which one does not love. / My faith is the / tenderness of your gazes. / Your faith / is in the words that I seek."

18. See the poem "A Giuliano Ferrara," at http://lapoesiaelospirito .wordpress.com/ 2008/05/08/sandro-bondi-perdonare-dio.

19. Andrea Vantini, *A Silvio*, at http://www.youtube.com/watch?v= SK1SCEbZHOA.

20. Baldesar Castiglione, *The Book of the Courtier* (*The Singleton Translation*), vol. 2, 18, New York, W.W. Norton, 2002, p. 80.

21. Plutarch, *Come distinguere l'adulatore dall'amico* (How to Tell a Flatterer from a Friend), ed. Alessandra Lukinovich and Madeleine Rousset with a preface by Luciano Canfora, Palermo, Sellerio, 1991, p. 41. English translation from http://www.bostonleadershipbuilders.com/plutarch/ moralia/how_to_tell_a_flatterer_from_a_friend.htm.

22. Thomas More, *Utopia*, in *The Complete Works of St. Thomas More*, ed. Edward Surz, S. J. Hexter, and Jack H. Hexter, New Haven, CT, Yale University Press, 1965, vol. IV, p. 57.

23. The quotations of Tacitus are taken from Algernon Sidney, *Discourses concerning Government*, ed. Thomas G. West, Indianapolis, Liberty Fund, 1990, pp. 271.

24. Vittorio Feltri, "Il Cavaliere in sedici scene," in *Berlusconi tale e quale: Vita, conquiste, battaglie, e passioni di un uomo politico unico al mondo*, Milan, Libero, 2009.

25. Maurizio Belpietro, *Editoriale: Perché Indro ruppe col Cav.*, *Panorama*, 6 May 2009.

26. Sidney, *Discourses concerning Government*, p. 254.

27. Ibid., p. 255.

28. Gianni Barbacetto, Peter Gomez, and Marco Travaglio, *Mani sporche*, Milan, Chiarelettere, 2007, pp. 746–47.

29. See http://leg15.camera.it/resoconti/dettaglio_resoconto.asp?idSed uta=198&resoconto=stenografico&tit=00090&fase.

30. Niccolò Machiavelli, *Florentine Histories*, trans. Harvey C. Mansfield and Laura F. Banfield, Princeton, Princeton University Press, 1988, p. 110.

31. I found this information in Peter Gomez and Marco Travaglio, *Se li conosci li eviti: Raccomandati, riciclati, condannati, imputati, ignoranti, voltagabbana, fannulloni del nuovo parlamento*, Milan, Chiarelettere, 2008, pp. 140–41.

32. Ibid., p. 143.

33. Barbacetto, Gomez, and Travaglio, *Mani sporche*, p. 382.

34. Ibid., pp. 28–31.

35. Ibid., p. 52.

Notes to Chapter Four

1. Giacomo Leopardi, *Discorso sopra lo stato presente dei costumi degl'Italiani*, in *Tutte le opere*, ed. Walter Binni, with the cooperation of Enrico Ghidetti, Florence, Sansoni, 1969, vol. I, p. 975.

2. Ibid., p. 981.

3. I quote from Norberto Bobbio, *Italia civile: Ritratti e testimonianze*, Florence, Passigli Editori, 1986, p. 97.

4. Carlo Rosselli, *Liberal Socialism*, ed. Nadia Urbinati, trans. William McCuaig, Princeton, Princeton University Press, 1994, p. 103. First Rosselli quote translated by Antony Shugaar.

5. Ernesto Rossi, *"Nove anni sono molti": Lettere dal carcere 1930–1939*, ed. Mimmo Franzinelli, Turin, Bollati Boringhieri, 2001, pp. 716–17; Rossi quotes translated by Antony Shugaar, with English-language translations of the biblical passages coming from the King James Bible.

6. Gaetano Salvemini, *Stato e Chiesa in Italia*, in *Opere di Gaetano Salvemini*, 2, *Scritti di Storia moderna e contemporanea*, vol. 3, Milan, Feltrinelli, 1969, p. 436.

7. J.C.L. Simonde de Sismondi noted this at the turn of the nineteenth century in his influential *Histoire des républiques italiennes du Moyen Age*, Paris, chez Treuttel et Würtz libraires, 1826, chap. 127, pp. 422–23.

8. Gaetano Salvemini, *Cattolicismo e democrazia*, in *Opere di Gaetano Salvemini*, II, *Scritti di Storia moderna e contemporanea*, vol. 3, p. 381.

9. Gaetano Mosca, *The Ruling Class*, trans. Hannah D. Kahn, New York, McGraw-Hill, 1939, p. 50.

10. Ibid., p. 53.

11. Nancy Bermeo, *Ordinary Citizens in Extraordinary Times: The Citizenry and the Breakdown of Democracy*, Princeton, Princeton University Press, 2003, pp. 51–2.

12. Ibid., p. 241.

13. Ibid., pp. 239–40.

14. Giuseppe Fiori, *Il venditore: Storia di Silvio Berlusconi e della Fininvest*, Milan, Garzanti, 2004, pp. 115–16.

15. Ibid., p. 114.

16. Ibid., pp. 180–81.

17. Ibid., pp. 175–76.

18. *L'Unità*, 23 March 1994.

19. Ibid., 19 February 1994.

20. Ibid., 6 March 1996.

21. Ibid., 23 March 1994.

22. Ibid., 30 March 1994.

23. Norberto Bobbio, *Grandi speranze, grandi timori*, in *Tra due repubbliche: Alle origini della democrazia italiana*, with a historical note by Tommaso Greco, Rome, Donzelli, 1996, pp. 134–35.

24. Ibid., p. 135.

25. See Paolo Sylos Labini, *Berlusconi e gli anticorpi: Diario di un cittadino indignato*, Rome-Bari, Laterza, 2003, pp. 47 and 63.

26. Ibid., p. 50.

27. Ibid., pp. 59–60.

28. Peter Gomez and Marco Travaglio, *Se li conosci li eviti*, Milan, Chiarelettere, 2008, pp. 375–76.

29. *L'Unità*, 7 February 2005.

30. *Il Corriere della Sera*, 15 July 2009.

Notes to Chapter Five

1. Vincenzo Gioberti, *Del rinnovamento civile dell'Italia*, ed. Luigi Quattrocchi, 3 vol., Rome, Abete, 1969, book 2, vol. 2, pp. 60–61.

2. Benedetto Croce, *Poeti e scrittori del pieno e del tardo Rinascimento*, 2d ed., Bari, Laterza, 1958, vol. 1, pp. 16 and 10. See in this connection the lovely pages by Carlo Ossola, *Dal "Cortegiano" all'"uomo di mondo,"* Turin, Einaudi, 1995, pp. 155–181

3. Paul Ginsborg, *Berlusconi: Ambizioni patrimoniali in una democrazia mediatica*, Turin, Einaudi, 2003, pp. 58–60.

4. Stefano Passigli, *Democrazia e conflitto di interessi. Il caso italiano: Conversazione con Renzo Cassigoli*, Milan, Ponte alle Grazie, 2001, pp. 32–33, but see also pp. 37–40 and the documentation on pp. 145–69.

5. I am quoting from Corrado Stajano, *Un eroe borghese: Il caso dell'avvocato Giorgio Ambrosoli assassinato dalla mafia politica*, Turin, Einaudi, 1991, pp. 102–3.

6. Guido Calogero, *Filosofia del dialogo*, Milan, Comunità, 1962, p. 105.

7. Concerning the nostalgia for the way of life of the servant, see Michael Walzer, *Exodus and Revolution*. New York, Basic Books, 1985.

8. English quote comes from R. Lubbers, W. van Genugten, and T. Lambooy, "Inspiration for Global Governance," at http://books.google.com/books?id=g842VTscInEC&pg=PA88&lpg=PA88&dq=gandhi+letter+to+julian+huxley&source=bl&ots=R3NLkaW7db&sig=Yiz4eHy4PBWCGglJZ6GPu9Sa5GY&hl=en&ei=hpNqTZHgN8aAlAflyrz_AQ&sa=X&oi=book_result&ct=result&resnum=1&ved=0CBsQ6AEwAA#v=onepage&q=gandhi%20letter%20to%20julian%20huxley&f=false.

9. Giuseppe Mazzini, *A Francesco Crispi* (1864), in *Scritti politici*, ed. Terenzio Grandi and Augusto Comba, Turin, UTET, 1972, pp. 969–70.

10. Massimo Mila, *Verdi*, ed. Piero Gelli, Milan, Rizzoli, 2000, pp. 194–95.

11. Amelia Rosselli, *Memorie*, ed. Marina Calloni, Bologna, il Mulino, 2001, pp. 47–48.

12. When his lawyer suggested that he ask Il Duce to grant clemency, Carlo Rosselli replied from the Como prison:

> But was the involvement [of the lawyer] really necessary? Couldn't we have communicated our refusal through the uncle [Salvemini] immediately? Saying *no* is itself prejudicial, any questions of merit aside. If they had asked me to love my wife and my mother, I would have shown the same attitude. I don't want to have any part in acknowledging any attenuation of my rights. Certainly, given the times we live in, it isn't easy to adhere to such a rigid standard of conduct; and there are times when I wonder whether by chance we aren't exaggerating; but I always come to the same conclusion. However my personal and collective adventure may end, I want to emerge with my moral capital intact. I reject therefore all forms of warranty, commitment, or mortgage.

A few days later, he wrote another letter to reject once again his lawyer's suggestions that he promise his future good conduct, which would have meant abandoning the struggle against Fascism:

> When you agree to undertake a tacit transaction you start down a terrible slippery slope; it's impossible to stop the downward momentum; all limitations are lost, everything seems legitimate. I know that *almost everyone* in my position would have acted (and in practical terms, *have acted*) differently; even the best. I know that in the times we live in, all

unilateral commitments are undermined by the weakness of obligation. I know something else: the day may well come when I may even almost regret being so obstinate. But the die is cast and there is no point in feeling regret. Let me say again that I sense, instinctively, that the example is only useful if it is pure, perfect, uncontaminated, only if it clearly demonstrates that there was someone who was able to follow, in spite of everything, a line of morality, of absolute intransigence.

I Rosselli: Epistolario familiare, 1914–1937, ed. Zeffiro Ciuffoletti, Milan, Mondadori, 1997, p. 332.

13. Ernesto Rossi, *Elogio della galera: Lettere, 1930–1943*, Bari, Laterza, 1968, pp. 62–63.

14. Ferruccio Parri, "Lettera al giudice istruttore di Savona," in *Scritti 1915/1975*, ed. Enzo Collotti, Giorgio Rochat, Gabriella Solaro Pelazza, and Paolo Speziale, Milan, Feltrinelli, 1976, pp. 63–64.

15. Giovanni Sartori, *Homo videns*, Rome-Bari, Laterza, 2000.

16. Tullio De Mauro, *La cultura degli italiani*, ed. Francesco Erbani, Rome-Bari, Laterza, 2004, pp. 162–63.

17. Francesca Rigotti, *L'onore degli onesti*, Milan, Feltrinelli, 1998.

18. Michel Foucault, *Sorvegliare e punire: nascita della prigione*, Turin, Einaudi, 1993.

19. Guido Calogero, *La scuola dell'uomo*, ed. Paolo Bagnoli, Reggio Emilia, Diabasis, 2003, pp. 31–32.

20. Diego Gambetta and Gloria Origgi, *L-worlds: The Curious Preference for Low Quality and Its Norms*, Oxford Series of Working Papers in Linguistics, 2009, 1.

21. It is worth recalling the famous words that Thucydides put in the mouth of Pericles: "We cultivate refinement without extravagance." Thucydides, *The History of the Peloponnesian War*, trans. Richard Crawley, Everyman's Library, London, E. M. Dent, 1914, p. 123.

22. Benedetto Croce, *History of Europe in the Nineteenth Century*, trans. Henry Furst, New York, Harcourt Brace, 1933, p. 360.

23. Norberto Bobbio, *Italia civile: Ritratti e testimonianze*, Florence, Passigli, 1986, pp. 286–87.

24. Ibid., pp. 132 and 128.

Index